A WOMAN'S WALK WITH GOD

A Daily Guide for Prayer and Spiritual Growth

SHEILA CRAGG

CROSSWAY BOOKS • WHEATON, ILLINOIS
A DIVISION OF GOOD NEWS PUBLISHERS

A Woman's Walk With God
Copyright © 1996 by Sheila Cragg

Published By:
Crossway Books
A division of Good News Publishers
1300 Crescent Street
Wheaton, Illinois 60187
All rights reserved.

Printed in the Republic of Singapore

ISBN 981-3087-30-7

ValuPrint Edition 1997 by
AENON INTERNATIONAL PTE LTD,
49 Jalan Pemimpin #03-06/07,
APS Industrial Building, Singapore 577203.

This **ValuPrint** edition published by arrangement
with Good News Publishers.

Editor: Lila Bishop

Cover design and illustration: Cindy Kiple

First printing 1996

Most Scripture in the prayers in this book is paraphrased from the versions listed
below, with some also from the *Amplified Bible*. Scripture quoted directly is
handled as follows:

Unless otherwise designated, Scripture is taken from the *Holy Bible: New International
Version*®NIV®. Copyright © 1973, 1978, 1984 by International Bible Society. Used by
permission of Zondervan Publishing House. All rights reserved.

The "NIV" and "New International Version" trademarks are registered in the United
States Patent and Trademark Office by International Bible Society. Use of either
trademark requires the permission of International Bible Society.

Verses marked TLB are taken from *The Living Bible* © 1971. Used by permission of
Tyndale House Publishers, Inc., Wheaton, IL 60189. All rights reserved.

Scripture quotations taken from the *Revised Standard Version* are identified RSV.
Copyright 1946, 1953 © 1971, 1973 by the Division of Christian Education of the
National Council of Churches in the USA.

Scripture from the King James Version is marked KJV.

Library of Congress Cataloging-in-Publication Data
Cragg, Sheila, 1938–
    A woman's walk with God : a daily guide for prayer and spiritual
growth / Sheila Cragg.
        p.   cm.
    Includes bilbliographical references and indexes.
    1. Women—Prayer-books and devotions—English.   2. Devotional
calendars.   1. Title.
BV4527.C715 1996   242'.643—dc20   95-46385
    ISBN 0-89107-875-4

04	03	02	01	00	99	98	97	96
15	14	13	12	11	10	9	8	7	6	5	4	3	2	1

To Ron, my beloved husband,
and Leona Ross, my dearest friend,
who have supported me and held me accountable
by their faithful prayers, steadfast love,
and spiritual wisdom

To the women of Nutwood Street Baptist Church
and Pine Grove Baptist Church
who attended the Deepening Your Devotional Life classes
and contributed so much to this book
by their encouragement, godliness,
and transparency

CONTENTS

ACKNOWLEDGMENTS

My deep appreciation goes to Lane Dennis and Leonard Goss whose commitment to publishing this book encouraged me at a time when I so greatly needed it. God's divine timing is amazing. I am thankful for Lila Bishop's gentleness, kindness, and perceptive suggestions as she edited this book. I have especially enjoyed working with her.

I appreciate the warm and gracious staff at Crossway, from the people who answer the phone to those who have contributed to the designing, publishing, and marketing of this book. I'm also grateful for the women at Pine Grove Baptist Church who proofread portions of the book.

I cannot begin to name or thank the many Christian friends, missionaries, pastors, and humble servants of God who have ministered to me, and who by their godliness have challenged me to remain committed in my own walk with Christ.

I am constantly grateful for the Word of God that convicts, enriches, and nourishes me and speaks to my concerns in uncountable ways. I want to thank the authors of the many books that have shaped my life spiritually; their books are very much a part of the fabric of mine.

Now to the One who is the Beginning and the End, to our ever-loving Lord, I give the praise, honor, and glory.

INTRODUCTION

$\mathcal{T}$his book was written for those who hunger for a devotional life that ministers to their hearts and meets personal spiritual needs. It was written to encourage us where we are—not where we ought to be in our spiritual journey. It was written to offer grace to those of us who have struggled with our quiet time and come away feeling guilt and failure rather than being renewed and strengthened in our faith. It was written that we might have a greater sense of the Lord's ever-loving presence in the painful times we're living in.

We'll discover what it means to have a devotional lifestyle rather than a regimented quiet time. This book is filled with creative, practical ways we can deepen our relationship with the Lord and strengthen our trust in Him during tough times.

A Woman's Walk with God can be used by individuals or small groups. It's a combination how-to and devotional. Every week includes a chapter covering the spiritual life with seven days of brief devotionals on the same theme. The opening page for each week has a Scripture passage to memorize during the week.

The daily devotionals include Scripture passages, lined spaces to write answers and thoughts about your spiritual life, and a personalized Scripture prayer. (I've personalized Scripture from various Bible versions by using the pronouns I, me, and my—and by putting the verses in my own words. Then these Scriptures are to be prayed back to the Lord. Scripture personalized or quoted directly is taken from the *Holy Bible: New International Version* unless otherwise marked.) And finally there are more spaces for the reader to record "Praises, Prayers, and Personal Notes."

Before you start reading each day's devotional, write the date on the blank line at the top of the page. Later you may want to reread what you've written. The date will help you relate that time to the events and concerns you were experiencing during that period. You will be able to compare where you were on your spiritual journey at that time and how you have progressed since then.

The first part, "Discovering the Devotional Life," includes Christ's call to come to Him for rest and spiritual renewal. The following weeks discuss the purposes for spending time with our Lord, the pattern Christ set for us, creative ideas for having devotions, and ways to keep a devotional journal.

The second part, "Developing the Disciplined Life," explains the meaning of the spiritual disciplines, praying to fortify our faith, learning Scripture, pursuing holiness, practicing God's presence, presenting ourselves for service, and pressing on in painful circumstances.

The third part, "Deepening the Spiritual Life," closes with guidelines for preparing a devotional retreat for spiritual renewal. It also provides retreat plans to follow.

It is my desire that all who use this book may come away spiritually satisfied and strengthened, may be refreshed and restored anew, and may come to know our caring Lord as a beloved companion.

PART ONE

Discovering the Devotional Life

WEEK ONE

Prepare to Rest

*"Come to me, all you who are weary
and burdened, and I will give you rest.
Take my yoke upon you and learn from me,
for I am gentle and humble in heart,
and you will find rest for your souls.
For my yoke is easy and my burden is light."*

MATTHEW 11:28-30

*O*ne summer afternoon a light wind waltzed across the lake, gliding along the glassy surface, dancing over the whitecapped surf, ruffling lavender lupines in the meadow. On nearby pines, the needles hummed softly in the breeze while the waves played up and down the sandy shore.

Creation's concert delighted my heart that day as I sat by the lake. I was touched by God's care for His smallest of creatures as I watched miniature insects scampering through the breeze-blown grasses. I was awed by God's majesty as I surveyed the magnificent mountain range. I wondered how God who reigns over a vast universe, the God who keeps track of planets billions of light-years apart, could so tenderly care for me.

I went to the lake that day because I desired a deeper relationship with the Lord and longed for a renewed sense of God's presence in my life. I needed rest from the relentless march of daily events. I yearned to find refuge from the constant cries of the telephone, the insistent demands of critical needs, and the shrill voices of a chaotic world. If only I could put aside the guilt of the "shoulds" and the demands of the undone; if only I could be freed for a few hours from the never-ending list of concerns.

My Creator Lord met my deepest desires for restoration that day. The restful sights and serene sounds soothed my weary heart. Breathing the air scented with pine and lake water, I felt as if I were inhaling His peaceful presence and exhaling my anxious concerns. In the sunlit surroundings, a thick fog of worries dissipated, fears evaporated, and frustrations vanished. He renewed my thirsting spirit as I drank in the tranquil setting, read my Bible, recorded deep-felt needs in my journal, and reflected on how I sensed His loving care for me.

Over the years, I've set specific times to go to an outdoor setting to strengthen my spiritual life. When I feel consumed by the cares of living and stress mounts its relentless attack, I seek the solitude of a lake or park. Beside gentle waters and grassy meadows, I spend restful hours alone with my Lord.

During those retreats to deepen my devotional life and in my regular quiet times with the Lord, I find physical restoration and spiritual renewal.

Jesus also went into the hills to find rest and spiritual refuge. Once when He was weary after ministering to the hungering crowds, He offered this invitation to His disciples: "'Come with me by yourselves to a quiet place and get some rest.' So they went away by themselves in a boat to a solitary place" (Mark 6:31-32).

All Who Are Weary and Burdened

In the same way Jesus calls us, "Come to me, all you who are weary and burdened, and I will give you rest. Take my yoke upon you and learn from me, for I am gentle and humble in heart, and you will find rest for your souls. For my yoke is easy and my burden is light" (Matthew 11:28-30).

Long ago I learned those verses without thinking of them as a personal invitation to find rest for my soul, to hear God with my heart, to listen to His Word until I found spiritual rest. I often questioned how Jesus' yoke could be easy to carry and His burden light when so much suffering and evil darkened our world. Then I came to realize that sin's heavy yoke overburdens us with guilt and shame, while Christ's light yoke redeems us with forgiveness and grace. God has assured us that "it is for freedom that Christ has set us free. Stand firm, then, and do not let yourselves be burdened again by a yoke of slavery" (Galatians 5:1).

Take off sin's yoke, the one that is rough, hard, and wearisome; put on the sacred yoke, the one that is pure, holy, and restful. "In repentance and rest is your salvation, in quietness and trust is your strength. . . . " (Isaiah 30:15).

The Lord is inviting us to find refuge in His caring presence when we're weary from our burdens, heavy-laden with anxiety, worn down by our troubles—troubles too heavy to bear alone.

I Will Give You Rest

Why does Christ ask us to come to Him when we're discouraged and overburdened rather than when we're rested? He invites us to come because He desires to refresh us spiritually. He desires to replenish and restore our faith.

He longs to give us relief from our physical, mental, and emotional pain. He longs to give us respite from unrelenting heartaches that exhaust us and allow us no reprieve.

Our Lord knows that we'll never feel fully at rest during our earthly journey. He knows that most of what we do daily to maintain our lives and much of what we do for pleasure leaves us tired. He knows that to escape our pain and those empty, lonely moments, we overload them with meaningless activities and anxious thoughts that fatigue us.

Christ calls us to come to Him when we're tired so He can give us rest from difficult human relationships and responsibilities, so He can relieve us of the burdens we bear, so He can refresh us when we're weary of the daily work we must do. "For anyone who enters God's rest also rests from his own work, just as God did from his. Let us, therefore, make every effort to enter that rest" (Hebrews 4:10-11).

Our loving Shepherd desires to lead us to green meadows beside still waters so He can cleanse our diseased thoughts, heal our damaged lives, and restore our souls. He longs to guide us through the valley of pain, to free us from the fear of evil, to comfort us with His rod and staff. He yearns to lead us along the path of righteousness for His name's sake.

The Lord Himself is inviting us to follow Him to a place of peaceful quietness for personal restoration, to find a place of solitude for spiritual recuperation. Come, sit at the place He's set for you. He longs to serve you, so let His healing Word quench your thirst; let His tender mercy refresh your starved soul; let His gracious love awaken your spiritual passion.

Scripture Reading: Genesis 2:1-2; Exodus 20:8-11

Practicing the Spiritual Life

God didn't need to rest after He created the earth, but by doing so He showed us the importance of resting from work. Why did God command us to rest?

_____

_____

_____

Often work, family responsibilities, and leisure activities so consume every moment that we become overly exhausted, and we miss our quiet time. Make a commitment to change your schedule this week. Set a specific time when you can meet with the Lord. Ask Him to give you physical rest and spiritual refreshment during your devotions.

_____

_____

_____

Prayer

Everlasting Lord, Creator of the ends of the earth, do I not know? Have I not heard? You do not grow tired or weary. You give strength to the weary and increase the power of the weak. When I grow tired and weary, and stumble and fall, I will hope in You, Lord, for You will renew my strength. Then I will soar on wings like an eagle; I will run and not grow weary; I will walk and not be faint. (Isa. 40:28-31 paraphrased)

Prayers, Praises, and Personal Notes

_____

_____

_____

Scripture Reading: Exodus 33:12-14

Practicing the Spiritual Life

Moses was fearful about doing God's will. What did Moses ask of God, and what did God promise in return?

_____

_____

_____

In what specific areas of your life do you need to find refuge in the same promise God gave Moses?

_____

_____

_____

Prayer

Lord God, my Protector, because I know Your name I will trust in You, for You have never forsaken those who seek You. Teach me the right way to live. Then my soul will find rest in You alone. I will trust in You at all times. I will pour out my heart to You, for You are my refuge. Hear my voice in accordance with Your love. O Lord, renew my life. (Ps. 9:10; 2 Chron. 6:26b; Ps. 62:1a, 8; 119:149 paraphrased)

Prayers, Praises, and Personal Notes

_____

_____

_____

_____

_____

_____

Scripture Reading: 2 Chronicles 14:2-7

Practicing the Spiritual Life
What did King Asa do to gain peace and rest?

_____

_____

_____

We experience personal peace and spiritual rest when we clear our lives of personal idols and offensive actions. Are there any altars or high places in your life that need to be removed so that you may gain peace? If so, ask the Lord to show you one idol that needs to be removed. Set a date and ask the Lord for strength to gain victory over it by that time.

_____

_____

_____

Prayer
Ever-forgiving Savior, I repent and turn to You so that my sins may be wiped out, so that times of refreshing may come from You. Each moment of the day help me to turn from evil and do good, to seek peace and pursue it. O Lord, may the fruit of righteousness in my life be peace; may the effect of righteousness be quietness and confidence forever. May I live in a peaceful dwelling place, in a secure home, in an undisturbed place of rest. (Acts 3:19; Ps. 34:14; Isa. 32:17-18 paraphrased)

Prayers, Praises, and Personal Notes

_____

_____

_____

_____

Scripture Reading: Jeremiah 6:16

Practicing the Spiritual Life
What does the Lord say we need to do to find rest for our souls?

_____

_____

_____

Ask the Lord to show you what new direction you need to walk in to find spiritual rest.

_____

_____

_____

Prayer
Lord, in my heart I plan my own course, but You determine my steps. I know, O Lord, that my life is not my own; it is not for me to direct my steps. Teach me to do Your will, for You are my God; may Your good Spirit lead me on level ground. Then I will know that I can set my heart at rest in Your presence. (Prov. 16:9; Jer. 10:23; Ps. 143:10; 1 John 3:19b paraphrased)

Prayers, Praises, and Personal Notes

_____

_____

_____

_____

_____

_____

_____

Scripture Reading: Psalm 91

Practicing the Spiritual Life

In this crime-ridden world we often fear the terrors of night and the arrows that fly at us by day. What does the Lord promise when we dwell in His shelter, rest in His shadow, and find refuge in Him?

_____

_____

_____

What concerns or fears do you have for which you need the Lord to be your refuge and fortress?

_____

_____

_____

Prayer

I will take refuge in You, Lord; let me never be put to shame; deliver me in Your righteousness. For the sake of Your name lead and guide me. Free me from the traps I've set for myself; be my refuge and safe haven. Hide me in the shelter of Your presence. You alone are my refuge and hiding place; protect me from trouble and surround me with songs of deliverance. (Ps. 31:1, 3b-4, 20a; 32:7 paraphrased)

Prayers, Praises, and Personal Notes

_____

_____

_____

_____

_____

Scripture Reading: Psalm 116:1-7

Practicing the Spiritual Life

Sorrow and trials often entangle us like the cords of death. How do we find spiritual rest during such painful difficulties?

_____

_____

_____

Where do you feel the greatest need for the Lord's gracious compassion and protection?

_____

_____

_____

Prayer

Lord, let Your hand rest on me. Then I will not turn away from You; revive me, and I will call on Your name. Restore me, O Lord God Almighty; make Your face shine upon me that I may be saved. As Your beloved child I will rest secure in You, for You shield me all day long, and because of Your love for me I will rest between Your shoulders. (Ps. 80:17a, 18-19; Deut. 33:12 paraphrased)

Prayers, Praises, and Personal Notes

_____

_____

_____

_____

_____

_____

Scripture Reading: Hebrews 4:1-11

Practicing the Spiritual Life

In the above passage, God is speaking about both present and future rest. What prevents us from finding God's rest?

_____

_____

_____

In what areas of your life do you need to make every effort to obey the Lord and enter into His rest?

_____

_____

_____

Prayer

Ever-living God, by Your strength I will see to it that I do not have a sinful, unbelieving heart that turns away from You. But I will encourage others, and may they encourage me so that we do not become hardened by sin's deceitfulness. Today, Jesus, I will hear Your voice. I will not harden my heart or become rebellious. My soul will find rest in You alone; for my hope comes from You. I will have the faith of God's elect and the knowledge of the truth that leads to godliness—a faith and knowledge resting on the hope of eternal life, which You, who do not lie, promised from the beginning of time. (Heb. 3:12-13, 15; Ps. 62:5; Titus 1:1b-2 paraphrased)

Prayers, Praises, and Personal Notes

_____

_____

_____

_____

WEEK TWO

Purpose to Deepen
Your Devotional Life

"Love the Lord your God
with all your heart
and with all your soul
and with all your strength."

DEUTERONOMY 6:5

*F*itness experts urge us to exercise to preserve our health. Regular exercise lowers harmful cholesterol levels and high blood pressure, burns off calories, increases stamina, and tones the body.

I walk for ten minutes a day. An exercise enthusiast would think my program was fairly useless. A ten-minute stroll through the supermarket would do just as well. Surprisingly, my brief exercising is essential to my well-being. Walking increases my energy and overcomes depression induced by medication for a sleep disorder. The same is true of my devotional life. If I miss my time with the Lord, I really feel the difference. Quiet time is essential to my spiritual well-being. My faith is increased and worry reduced.

The ten-minute exerciser and the fitness club addict who spends hours at a gym would give different reasons for the amount of time they spend working out. The same is true for our devotional life. Some people feel that a ten-minute devotional is enough while others feel that an hour is too brief.

The way one begins a new exercise program is the way to begin our devotional life. It works best to start out slowly. Personal transformation comes through a gradual but consistent commitment to daily exercising our faith and spiritually working through concerns with our Lord. An excess of enthusiasm and a lack of consistency will only defeat and discourage us. Then we won't reach our goal to become spiritually fit servants of Christ.

Fatigue also hinders our motivation to exercise. Before we start, we may feel so tired we don't think we have enough energy, but once we begin exercising, our strength begins to build. Often I feel that way when I start my devotions. I'm so tired and barely awake enough to focus on the words—let alone concentrate on their meaning. But by the time I'm finished, I'm awake, refreshed, and amazed at the many ways the Lord has spoken to me and prepared me to serve Him during that day.

Every good exercise program outlines sound reasons for working out according to a specific plan. Knowing why exercise is important to maintaining good health, however, is useless if we lack the interest.

We may also know all the reasons why we need to maintain spiritual health, but we lack the motivation. Often we need to begin the habit of having a quiet time by praying for the desire.

If we have a negative view about exercise or just plain don't enjoy doing it, we won't do it. We may decide it's too boring. We don't have time. We really don't care. We have more important things to do. Or we may think we want to exercise, but we allow other priorities to interfere. The same is true if we feel negative about a daily devotional workout. We'll also allow routine obligations to hinder us.

The benefits of all-around spiritual fitness will be achieved if we maintain consistency and self-discipline. Once we purpose to strengthen our devotional life, we'll experience the blessings of spending time with our Lord.

The Reason Is Love

What then are the basic reasons for spending quality time with our Lord, for building a spiritual exercise program? And where do we begin? *First, we begin with love.*

God's love is the deepest incentive and highest motive for developing a consistent devotional life. "Love the Lord your God with all your heart and with all your soul and with all your strength" (Deut. 6:5, 10:12; Matt. 22:37). "Be imitators of God, therefore, as dearly loved children and live a life of love, just as Christ loved us and gave himself up for us as a fragrant offering and sacrifice to God" (Eph. 5:1-2).

The second reason, stated ten different times throughout the Bible, is to "love your neighbor as yourself" (Lev. 19:18). The Lord not only directs us to love our neighbor, who may or may not believe in God, but the entire book of 1 John is a love commandment to Christians: "Love one another. . . . if we love one another, God lives in us and his love is made complete in us" (1 John 4:11-12).

Moreover, God compelled the Israelites to treat aliens as they would their native-born. "Love him as yourself, for you were aliens in Egypt" (Lev. 19:34). In the New Testament as well, the Lord directs us to show kindness to strangers (Matt. 25:35).

Loving others is often a difficult challenge, but the hardest of all is to "love your enemies and pray for those who persecute you" (Matt. 5:44). Hatred, prejudice, and judgmental attitudes repel and wound us and the people we dislike. Acceptance, compassion, and love compel us to act with the same grace, kindness, and mercy Jesus gives us.

"Above all, love each other deeply, because love covers over a multitude of sins" (1 Peter 4:8). God Himself commands us to love the Father, Son, and Holy Spirit, aliens and foreigners, Christians and non-Christians, enemies and opponents, family members and friends, neighbors and strangers. Our quiet times afford us the opportunity for the Lord to build love for others into our hearts, minds, and actions.

Love, however, doesn't come easily or naturally. When we meet with our Lord, we can pour out our struggles to love people who hurt us and who behave in destructive ways. We can freely ask the Lord to show us how to love our neighbors whom we may not even know. We can ask Him to show us how to love others while disagreeing with their choices, how to love those who wound us deeply, how to love prodigals who have become distant from us and their heavenly Father who loves them and watches with us for their return.

Though love is what Christ calls us to, we need to give ourselves the grace to realize that He alone can give us that loving compassion for the unlovable people in our lives. During our quiet times, He is able to heal our pain and enable us to love when we don't feel we have any to give. Like the father of the prodigal, we may need to release our loved ones who have gone their own way and pour out our love for them through prayer.

The Purposes Are Confession, Prayer, and Service

The second reason for devotions summons us to keep short accounts, to confess and be freed from our sins so that we might have a clean heart and a right spirit before our Lord.

Third, our time with the Lord gives us the opportunity to pray consistently, worship, and praise Him. God also desires that we listen to His Spirit, seek and experience His guidance, and ask for spiritual wisdom, understanding, and insights regarding our daily life and relationships with others.

Through prayer and reading the Word, we're gradually transformed, and our minds are renewed. We become more pure and holy of mind and heart, and we grow in the fruit of the Spirit.

Another reason why we need to develop spiritually is so we can "serve one another in love" (Gal. 5:13). "Each one should use whatever gift he has received to serve others, faithfully administering God's grace in its various forms" (1 Peter 4:10).

The Ultimate Goal Is Spiritual Rest and Fitness

As we faithfully meet with Jesus, He helps us face trials of all kinds, receive comfort and strength, and He enables us to comfort others in their troubles. During tough times, we learn to trust Him more and more. Our faith is strengthened; we experience spiritual refreshment, establish constancy in our journey, and become more aware of His caring presence.

God compels us to strengthen our spiritual life. The goal of all spiritual training is to become fit servants of Christ, to become more and more like Him. He is able to preserve our spiritual well-being; reduce harmful attitudes and actions; burn off anger, bitterness, and other destructive thoughts; tone our faith, and increase our energy and enthusiasm to serve Him.

Athletes train for thousands of hours for four or more years to compete in one event—the Olympics. They strive to win the gold. God desires that we strive to earn a heavenly gold medal. To do so, God urges us to train here on earth so we can earn faith-winning medals before we cross that heavenly finish line.

Scripture Reading: Deuteronomy 6:4-9; Matthew 22:37-39

Practicing the Spiritual Life

According to both the Old and New Testaments, the primary reason for developing a devotional life is to love our Lord and others. How and with whom are we to share His love and His Word?

_____

_____

_____

Ask the Lord to show you specific ways to express love to one person you find difficult to care about. Make a commitment this week to demonstrate love to that person in specific ways.

_____

_____

_____

Prayer

Ever-loving Lord, help me to love others, for love comes from You. When I am loving, gracious Father, I am born of You, and I know You. When I am unloving, I fail to demonstrate that I know You, Lord, for You are Love. This is true love: not that I loved You, God, but that You loved me and sent Your Son as an atoning sacrifice for my sins. Jesus, I love You because You first loved me. But if I say, "I love You, Lord," and yet hate my brothers and sisters, I am a liar. For if I don't love those I see and know, I cannot love You, God, whom I haven't seen. I will follow Your command. I will love You, Lord, and I will love my brothers and sisters. (1 John 4:7-8, 10, 19-21 paraphrased)

Prayers, Praises, and Personal Notes

_____

_____

Scripture Reading: Psalm 51:1-17; 1 John 1:5–2:6

Practicing the Spiritual Life

Confession of sin is a major reason for having devotions. What has Jesus done for us, and what does He continue to do?

_____

_____

_____

We're often blind to our sins and in denial about what we're doing wrong. We also downplay the seriousness and damaging consequences to ourselves and others. Admission, confession, and repentance are the three steps to overcoming sin. Repentance releases us from the bondage of guilt and shame. Ask the Lord to reveal areas of sin in your life, remembering that He desires to deliver and transform us by His tender mercy.

_____

_____

_____

Prayer

Ever-forgiving Savior, my guilt has overwhelmed me like a burden too heavy to bear. By concealing my sins, I do not spiritually prosper. But I will confess my sins and renounce them that I may obtain Your mercy. For who is a God like You who pardons my sin and forgives my transgressions? You do not stay angry forever but delight to show mercy. Lord, have compassion on me. Tread my sins underfoot and hurl all my iniquities into the depths of the sea. (Ps. 38:4; Prov. 28:13; Mic. 7:18-19 paraphrased)

Prayers, Praises, and Personal Notes

_____

_____

_____

Scripture Reading: Ephesians 6:18-20

Practicing the Spiritual Life

Prayer and praise are foundational to our devotional life. How are we to pray, and for whom should we pray?

_____

_____

_____

Ask the Lord to show you whom to pray for this week. Record their names and daily intercede for them.

_____

_____

_____

Prayer

Lord, teach me to devote myself to prayer, being watchful and thankful. I kneel before You, Father God, from whom Your whole family in heaven and on earth derives its name. I pray that out of Your glorious riches You may strengthen the people I'm holding up before You with power through Your Spirit in their inner being, so that Christ may dwell in their hearts through faith. And I pray that they may be rooted and established in love. (Col. 4:2; Eph. 3:14-17 paraphrased)

Prayers, Praises, and Personal Notes

_____

_____

_____

_____

_____

Scripture Reading: Psalm 119:1-11, 33-40

Practicing the Spiritual Life

Another reason for having devotions is to spend time reading and listening to God's Word, seeking His wisdom and spiritual guidance, and following His direction for our daily lives. How are we to apply the Word of God to our lives?

Record how the Lord speaks to you about following His guidance more closely.

Prayer

O that my soul may be consumed with longing for Your laws at all times, Lord God. Let me understand the teaching of Your precepts; then I will meditate on Your wonders. Strengthen me according to Your Word. Keep me from deceitful ways; be gracious to me through Your law. I have chosen the way of truth; I have set my heart on Your laws. I am holding fast to Your statutes. (Ps. 119:20, 27, 28b-31a paraphrased)

Prayers, Praises and Personal Notes

Scripture Reading: Romans 8:5-6; 12:1-2

Practicing the Spiritual Life

We meet with the Lord so He can change us into His image. What does the Lord promise when we come before Him so that He might renew our minds and transform our lives?

_____

_____

_____

Ask the Lord to reveal specific actions that need to be changed so that He may transform you. What habits of thinking do you need to change so that you can set your mind on what the Spirit desires?

_____

_____

_____

Prayer

Jesus, You have been teaching me in regard to my former way of life to put off my old self, which is corrupted by deceitful desires, to be made new in the attitude of my mind and to put on a new self, created to be like You in true righteousness and holiness. Lord, give me a new heart and put a new spirit within me; remove from me a heart of stone and give me a heart of flesh. Fill me with Your Spirit and move me to follow Your decrees and to be careful to keep Your laws. For Your eyes range throughout the earth to strengthen those whose hearts are fully committed to You. (Eph. 4:22-24; Ezek. 36:26-27; 2 Chron. 16:9 paraphrased)

Prayers, Praises, and Personal Notes

_____

_____

_____

Scripture Reading: Philippians 2:3-8; 1 Peter 4:8-11

Practicing the Spiritual Life

By spending time with our Lord, we learn how to serve Him. With what attitude and actions are we to serve our Lord?

_____

_____

_____

Often we think of serving the Lord as a major project rather than daily discovering how we can please Him in our relationships and in our ordinary tasks. Ask the Lord to show you how you can serve Him and others in one simple way this week.

_____

_____

_____

Prayer

Son of Man, You came not to be served, but to serve and to give Your life a ransom for many. Enable me to serve You with all my heart and all my soul. Show me how to serve others in love. Since You have given me freedom, but not the freedom to be selfish and serve myself, I will use my freedom to love and serve others. (Matt. 20:28; Josh. 22:5b; Gal. 5:13 TLB paraphrased)

Prayers, Praises, and Personal Notes

_____

_____

_____

_____

Scripture Reading: James 5:7-11

Practicing the Spiritual Life

We faithfully meet with the Lord to be spiritually strengthened so we can endure hardships. What are some of the ways we are to stand firm in all kinds of situations and trials?

_____

_____

_____

Do you need the Lord's strength to help you be patient, stand firm, and persevere in trials you may be going through? If so, what are those trials?

_____

_____

_____

Prayer

Lord God, set my feet on a rock and give me a firm place to stand on. Help me to show earnestness by trusting in the full assurance of hope until the end, so that I may not be spiritually sluggish, but an imitator of those who through faith and by practice of patient endurance and waiting inherit the promises. For I need endurance, so that I may do Your will and receive what is promised. Deliver me from drawing back and shrinking in fear, for then You will have no delight or pleasure in me. But may I be among the just and righteous servants who live by faith in You. (Ps. 40:2b; Heb. 6:11-12; 10:36, 38b, 38a RSV and AMP paraphrased)

Prayers, Praises, and Personal Notes

_____

_____

_____

_____

Pattern Your Life After Christ's

"I am the vine; you are the branches.
If a man remains in me and I in him,
he will bear much fruit;
apart from me you can do nothing."

JOHN 15:5

*V*ineyards grow and flourish in the hot, dry land of Israel and were often used as metaphors in Scripture to illustrate how people may grow spiritually into luscious fruit or sour, bitter grapes. In *The Song of the Vineyard* in Isaiah 5:1-7, God speaks of His great love for His people and how He especially chose them as He would fertile land for a vineyard.

In the earth of their lives, He tried to plant His Word so they would bear an abundant harvest of fruit. He attempted to dig out and clear their minds and hearts of the stones of sin. He built a watchtower so He could protect and watch over His people.

Then God waited and "looked for a crop of good grapes, but it yielded only bad fruit." God questioned, "What more could have been done for my vineyard than I have done for it? When I looked for good grapes, why did it yield only bad?"

Through the biblical imagery of a vineyard, we see God's great care, preparation, and work in our lives so that we might bear an abundance of good fruit. He longs above all else that we may flourish in our faith. God will do everything to produce a harvest that will glorify Him. The choice is ours, however, whether we bear good or bad fruit.

Jesus often referred to the cultivation of grapes in His parables to illustrate how we're to pattern our lives after His. In John 15, He selects the grapevine to show His spiritual union with us. Jesus tells us how we're to bear fruit by remaining attached to the Vine, how we're to follow His commands and remain in His love just as He obeyed His Father's commands and remained in His love. Jesus demonstrates the pattern He set for His spiritual life as an example for our own.

Jesus is the Vine, and He desires that we grow into His fruit-bearing branches. He desires that we spiritually grow as tenaciously as spreading grapevines; their tightly curled tendrils grasp onto and scale high stone fences. The Lord yearns for us to clasp onto and climb the sheer walls of faith and commitment. Even when He prunes us, and the intense heat of trials beats on us as the noonday sun in summertime, He longs for us to continue bearing His good fruit.

Jesus' Devotional Pattern

Jesus remained in His Father's love by spending hours alone with Him. Jesus often withdrew to lonely places and prayed (Luke 5:1). "Very early in the morning, while it was still dark, Jesus got up, left the house and went off to a solitary place, where he prayed" (Mark 1:35). He retreated to the outdoors to pray and to prepare to do His Father's will. In the same way, Jesus calls us to go to a place of solitude for prayer and spiritual renewal. And the only way to be alone with Him is by removing ourselves from all distractions and other people.

To find time alone with the Lord, we may need to meet with Him in the early hours of the morning or at midday or late at night. Though I'm more of a night person, I'm too tired and forget to have devotions then, so I take time each morning.

Setting a certain time is essential in helping us become consistent. And daily consistency is as important as the amount of time we spend. Once I determined to be consistent, I developed a habit. Now I feel at a loss when I miss my devotions. I feel as if something is missing. I feel more at rest and at peace during the day when I meet with the Lord. I have a greater sense of His guiding presence.

If we daily spend ten to fifteen minutes with the Lord, He will meet with us and strengthen us spiritually. The time I spend with the Lord varies each day from about ten minutes to an hour or more. Often when I finish my devotions, I wish I could stay longer in His presence.

Spending some time with the Lord is better than none at all. It's true that the more we're with the Lord, the stronger we grow spiritually.

A Sacred Place

To come aside with the Lord, find one place that is not cluttered with things that demand your attention. Set aside a corner if that is all you have, and turn it into a sanctuary where you can meet the Lord. It can be a simple place. I have my devotions while sitting on my bed. My husband, Ron, has his devotional time in an overstuffed chair in the living room. We have set aside those places for meeting with the Lord.

Where and how we have our devotions has changed over the years, because our lives are constantly changing. The needs in our own lives and those in our families differ from day to day and year to year. We have no idea what we'll experience even in the next moment.

We have no idea what our real spiritual needs are; only the Lord truly knows what He desires to teach us. Since this is true, our devotional needs will change. How the Lord wants to guide us, what passage of Scripture or book or music or person He plans to use in our lives changes as our lives change.

It also takes creativity and flexibility to find new places and times to have our devotions. Where we meet with our Lord today will be quite different from where we spend it tomorrow. When our sons were growing up, the place and amount of time I spent with the Lord was far different from what it is now.

I've also experienced job changes from full- to part-time work. My part-time teaching schedule changes from year to year. As a result, the place, time, and how I have my devotions has changed. Now I teach at nights, and I'm able to have more leisurely devotions in the morning than when I started work at eight o'clock.

I begin my devotions in the morning when I first wake up. I also eat a piece of fruit so that I don't constantly think about being hungry. When I used to walk on a treadmill, I prayed, listened to hymns or praise music, read verse cards, and/or read a book.

If you can find a safe, parklike setting, having devotions outdoors is an especially wonderful way to get in touch with our Creator Lord. You don't have to contend with the phone and other interruptions. A friend of mine leaves for work early, sits in her car next to a park, and has devotions. When I had an earlier work schedule, I used to walk around the nearby elementary school grounds where I prayed and carried verse cards with me to reflect on and/or memorize. I called it my schoolyard sanctuary because graceful elm trees lined the perimeters, and in the early morning it was like a bird refuge.

I also have a half- or full-day retreat for spiritual renewal that especially makes a difference in my relationship with the Lord. I've also gone on two- or three-day retreats alone. During those retreats, I read and reflect on Scripture, reassess the course of my life, and seek spiritual refreshment. After a day of experiencing the life-changing presence of God, I desire to be with Him more and more.

Our Creator is the Master Gardener who desires to plant His Word in our lives. He desires that we pattern our life after Christ's by remaining attached to the Vine so that our branches may bear luscious fruit for Him to enjoy. He longs for us to establish a consistent quiet time so that He can prune out sin, cut off dead branches, cultivate the soil of our hearts, and tenderly nurture our growth. He yearns to meet with us in a simple, sacred place where we can spiritually flourish in His watchful, protecting presence.

Scripture Reading: John 15:1-17

Practicing the Spiritual Life

We pattern our spiritual life after Christ's by staying attached to the Vine. What are some of the promises Jesus gives us if we remain in Him?

_____

_____

_____

Is there any area of your life that is cut off from the Vine? In what areas would you like the Lord to strengthen your attachment to Him?

_____

_____

_____

Prayer

Lord, fill me with the wisdom that comes from heaven, which is first of all pure, then peace-loving, considerate, submissive, full of mercy and good fruit, impartial, and sincere. Enable me to live by the fruit of Your Spirit—by love, joy, peace, patience, kindness, goodness, faithfulness, gentleness, and self-control. Make me a peacemaker who sows in peace in order to raise a harvest of righteousness. Then I will be filled with the fruit of righteousness that comes through You, Jesus Christ, and to Your glory, honor, and praise, O God. (James 3:17; Gal. 5:22-23a; James 3:18; Phil. 1:11 paraphrased)

Prayers, Praises, and Personal Notes

_____

_____

_____

_____

_____

Scripture Reading: Psalm 5:1-3

Practicing the Spiritual Life

What was David's pattern for coming to the Lord? How often did David meet with Him?

_____

_____

_____

If you haven't set a consistent time for meeting with the Lord, ask Him to show you what will work best for you. Set a specific time, and ask for His help in being faithful to your commitment. If you have an established pattern already, are there any changes you feel impressed to make?

_____

_____

_____

Prayer

Lord God, I call to You evening, morning, and noon. I cry out in distress, and You hear my voice. I cast all my cares on You, for You never let the righteous fall. Your steadfast love never ceases; Your mercies never come to an end; they are new every morning; great is Your faithfulness. "The Lord is my portion," says my soul, "therefore I will hope in him." You are good to me when I wait for You and seek You with all my heart and soul. (Ps. 55:16-17, 22; Lam. 3:22-25 RSV paraphrased)

Prayers, Praises, and Personal Notes

_____

_____

_____

_____

Scripture Reading: Daniel 6:3-27

Practicing the Spiritual Life
What pattern and place did Daniel set for meeting with the Lord? How did he respond to the decree to worship the king?

_____

_____

_____

Meeting faithfully with the Lord when we experience opposition is very difficult. Opposition may come from others, but it may also come from our own nature fighting against us or a demanding work schedule and other pressing commitments. If this is a problem for you, ask the Lord to show you how you can consistently meet with Him despite conflicts and opposition.

_____

_____

Prayer
"Do not be far from me, for trouble is near, and there is no one to help." "But you, O Lord, be not far off; O my Strength, come quickly to help me." Rescue me from the hand of my enemy, and enable me to serve You without fear in holiness and righteousness before You all my days. I watch in hope for You, Lord; I wait for You, for You will hear me. I put my hope in You, for I will yet praise You, my Savior and my God. (Ps. 22:11, 19 not paraphrased; Luke 1:74-75; Mic. 7:7; Ps. 42:11b paraphrased)

Prayers, Praises, and Personal Notes

_____

_____

_____

Scripture Reading: Matthew 14:22-23; Luke 5:16

Practicing the Spiritual Life

Where did Jesus go when He needed to be alone with His Father, and what did He do during that time?

_____

_____

_____

To follow Christ's example, we need to think of creative ways to get away to be with Him. Set a specific date and hour to spend a longer period of time with Him. Write this appointment on your calendar. One hour can make a difference in strengthening your walk with God, a half or full day even more.

_____

_____

_____

Prayer

Who may ascend Your hill, O Lord? Who may stand in Your holy place? Where will wisdom be found? And where is the place of understanding? You understand the way to it, and You know its place. Lord, to fear You is wisdom, and to depart from evil is understanding. Show me the place where I can meet with You, where I can find Your wisdom and understanding. For You have promised to lead me in the way of wisdom and along straight paths. (Ps. 24:3; Job 28:12, 23, 28 RSV; Prov. 4:11 paraphrased)

Prayers, Praises, and Personal Notes

_____

_____

_____

_____

Scripture Reading: Mark 6:30-34; Luke 4:42-44

Practicing the Spiritual Life

What problems did Jesus encounter when He tried to get away to a quiet place? How did He handle the needs of the crowd?

_____

_____

_____

Do you struggle with trying to find time to meet with the Lord in the midst of many activities and people's needs? How does this passage speak to you about handling the unexpected needs of others?

_____

_____

_____

Prayer

"Listen to my prayer, O God, do not ignore my plea; hear me and answer me." "I said, 'Oh, that I had the wings of a dove! I would fly away and be at rest—I would flee far away and stay in the desert; I would hurry to my place of shelter, far from the tempest and storm.'" "Let the morning bring me word of your unfailing love, for I have put my trust in you. Show me the way I should go, for to you I lift up my soul." (Ps. 55:1-2a, 6-8; 143:8-9)

Prayers, Praises, and Personal Notes

_____

_____

_____

_____

_____

Scripture Reading: Mark 1:35-39

Practicing the Spiritual Life

Not only did the crowds disturb Jesus' time alone with His Father, but so did the disciples who were essentially His family. How did Jesus turn interruptions into opportunities?

_____

_____

_____

Ask the Lord to help you have more uninterrupted time with Him. Pray that He'll help you turn distractions into opportunities to share your faith with family and friends.

_____

_____

_____

Prayer

Lord, my times are in Your hands. Preserve our times together, for when I am with You, I learn wisdom, and from Your mouth come knowledge and understanding. Help me, Holy Counselor, to be wise in the way I act toward others, including outsiders, and to make the most of every opportunity. Teach me how to carry on conversations that are always full of grace and seasoned with salt, so that I may know how to answer everyone. (Ps. 31:15a; Col. 4:5-6; Prov. 2:6 paraphrased)

Prayers, Praises, and Personal Notes

_____

_____

_____

_____

Scripture Reading: Genesis 32:22-30; 35:9-14

Practicing the Spiritual Life

Jacob didn't choose the places where God met with him. God's appearances were unexpected. What did He ask of Jacob? What was Jacob's response after God spoke to him?

_____

_____

_____

It's essential that we establish a pattern and a place to meet with our Lord. But just as God surprised Jacob, He may speak to us at an unexpected time and place. Ask the Lord to speak to You through His Word and to help you hear and follow His guidance.

_____

_____

_____

Prayer

Lord, from heaven You look down and see all mankind; from Your dwelling place You watch all who live on earth—You who form the hearts of all, consider everything I do. Therefore, Lord God, I will listen to what You will say; for You promise peace to me when I do. I will listen to Your instruction and be wise; I will not ignore it. For You will bless me for listening to You, for watching daily at Your doors, for waiting at Your doorway. (Ps. 33:13-15; 85:8a; Prov. 8:33-34 paraphrased)

Prayers, Praises, and Personal Notes

_____

_____

_____

WEEK FOUR

Plan to Strengthen Your Spiritual Life

*"The plans of the Lord
stand firm forever,
the purposes of his heart
through all generations."*

PSALM 33:11

*A*larm buzzes. It's 5:50 A.M. Punch snooze button. Doze and wait for alarm to sound off again. Keep punching the button until my mind sets off its own alarm. Scurry out of bed. Grab my Bible. Have half a devotion. Put on my walking clothes. Walk twenty minutes. Eat. Shower. Dress. Grab a snack and my teaching materials. Hurry to the car. Rush off to work—late again.

Finish teaching. Check my to-do list. Rush to an appointment. Run errands. Squeeze one duty into the next until night. Collapse into bed. Another day is gone, and only a few meager moments were spent with my Lord.

Perhaps you're like me—you struggle to maintain a quality devotional life. I've gone spiritually hungry because I didn't think I had the time for devotions or because of apathy or guilt over sins I'd failed to conquer.

As I've disciplined myself to meet regularly with my Lord, He has satisfied my hunger and caused me to thirst for more. Our Lord asks us to come dine with Him as often as we eat regular meals, and He hasn't called us to go on a diet. He invites us to come to His banquet table: "Listen, listen to me, and eat what is good, and your soul will delight in the richest of fare. Give ear and come to me; hear me, that your soul may live" (Isa. 55:2b-3).

Just as it takes time to prepare for a grand banquet, it takes commitment to plan for and feed our spiritual lives. Eating with the Lord at His table is as satisfying as a gourmet feast. But instead of having a magnificent meal, we often settle for airy cotton-candy devotions that leave us empty and dissatisfied. When we don't take enough time with our Lord, we still feel hungry.

Open Hands, Open Heart

We need to feed ourselves spiritually, but our definition of devotions is often limited to setting aside a certain amount of time to read our Bible and pray. Through the years, I've changed my view of how we develop a spiritual life. I've become more relaxed and less rigid about my morning quiet time.

I make devotional plans with open hands and set spiritual disciplines with an open heart.

Since we have no idea what unexpected detour, sudden accident, or circuitous route awaits us on the roadway of life, we can't predict what will alter our direction. We're on a sacred journey we've never been on before—one that scales sheer-faced mountainsides, one that drifts into dry, dangerous deserts, one that winds into luxurious countrysides. We have no idea what divine appointments—either delightful serendipities or sudden disasters—await us.

God's ways of training us spiritually are not our ways; His ways of conditioning our faith are not ours. Because the way to a deeper spiritual life is often difficult, we falter at obstacles, stagger over heartaches, and stumble over hardships.

Sometimes the greater our pain, the weaker our faith. We don't understand why God doesn't intervene, why we have to live with a chronic problem or unrelenting heartache. We may even give up spiritually because we feel abandoned or become angry or depressed when there seems to be no hope and nothing changes.

We may be overloaded with guilt because of certain sins we can't overcome, and we give up and sit on the sidelines. But our Lord doesn't want us to sprint the spiritual race in shame. He wants us to run a lifelong marathon by grace—grace that cleanses us from sin, grace that frees us to run at a steady pace, grace that quenches our spiritual thirst, sweet grace that gives us an extra surge of energy. And when we trip over hurdles, we can trust the Lord's unfailing mercy to pick us up and help us keep going on the sweaty racetrack of life.

We always need to seek balance in our spiritual fitness-building program. We can become so rigid about our devotional life that we're inflexible or so flexible that we're undisciplined.

The Devotional Lifestyle

We're more likely to fail at devotions if we feel we're a spiritual failure. If we're inconsistent or rush through our time with the Lord, if we don't have devotions in a certain way or do them exactly like someone else, we feel defeated. If our mind wanders and we can't concentrate, if we don't get anything out of what we're reading and come away feeling dry and empty, we wonder: *Why bother?*

I used to feel as if I'd failed when I came away from my quiet time spiritually empty. I now realize that it takes more than reading the Bible or a devotional book. It takes a devotional plan that includes many ways to nurture and satisfy our spiritual hunger.

We also need to follow a plan that considers our commitments, interests, schedules, personal heartaches, and pressing needs. If we choose faith-building activities that meet our needs, we're more likely to maintain a consistent devotional life.

We must be wary, however, of developing a devotional life that only satisfies our own personal desires and doesn't allow the Lord to teach us how to be accountable, obedient, and transformed. "The Lord says: 'These people come near to me with their mouth and honor me with their lips, but their hearts are far from me'" (Isa. 29:13a). Ezekiel said, "My people come to you, as they usually do, and sit before you to listen to your words, but they do not put them into practice. With their mouths they express devotion, but their hearts are greedy for unjust gain. . . . for they hear your words but do not put them into practice" (Ezek. 33:31-32).

The Lord commends us to do more than have devotions. He calls us to practice obedience and demonstrate His presence in our lives and in all our relationships. The main reason for developing a devotional plan is to enable us to know and love Him so intimately that we can serve others in a godly, loving way.

Making a Devotional Plan

We can achieve spiritual stamina and fitness when we follow a plan that allows for a slow, steady, and balanced state of growth. But if we lead spiritually sedentary lives and don't do faith-building exercises, we become fatigued and out of shape.

Since we have different personalities, we'll become more committed to having a consistent quiet time if each person follows a plan geared to his or her needs. For example, my husband and I both read our Bibles along with other Christian books, but he prefers ones written in a popular style while I enjoy devotionals.

Consider the following questions as you pray about finding a plan that will work for you:

Do you prefer to do a Bible study or read a daily devotional and/or a Christian book written in an inspirational style? Would you rather read the

Bible alone? Maybe you'd prefer to read the Bible along with a wide variety of other books, commentaries, devotionals, or studies.

Do you enjoy reading how Scripture applies to your own life? Or do you prefer to study certain topics or do an overview study of the Bible? Do you enjoy discovering the meaning in a single verse or passage or doing a more detailed chapter-by-chapter or verse-by-verse analysis?

If you prefer Bible studies, do you like ones that are brief or ones that are long? Do you like studies written in an easy narrative or in a heavy theological style? Do you prefer studies that you just read or ones that require you to fill in answers?

You may enjoy the spiritual classics or a single-page devotional with a story you can apply to your life. Maybe you don't enjoy reading at all; you prefer to listen to Christian music, sermons, or Bible studies on the radio or cassette tapes.

Even after considering the above possibilities, you may not be sure what you prefer. (A recommended list of Bibles and books are included in this chapter.) Try different kinds of devotionals or studies until you discover the ones that convict and challenge and excite you to spend more time with our Savior and Lord.

Be creative in planning your devotional life. The different ways to strengthen your walk with God are numerous. Consistently following even the simplest of devotional suggestions along with other disciplines will increase your faith.

If you have children, it's important to make them part of your devotional life. We all need to spend time alone with the Lord, but when we read the Bible or devotional books to our children or do other types of faith-building activities with them, our own spirituality will be strengthened.

It's also essential to realize that it takes time to develop our spirituality, and as we pass through the seasons of our lives, what we need today is far different from what we'll need tomorrow. I've spent many years discovering ways to strengthen my spiritual life. You may have heard of some of the following suggestions but thought they were too simple. How could reading a daily Scripture calendar or selecting verse cards from a promise box make any difference? It's not doing one kind of exercise that helps us maintain spiritual fitness; it's doing many kinds of exercises.

When I was teaching part time in the morning, I began my devotional time as soon as I got up and continued until I arrived at the site where I taught English as a Second Language to adults. Here are some examples of how I built my devotional life: Upon waking, I read my Bible and devotional books and/or wrote in my spiritual journal for ten to twenty minutes.

While I walked for exercise in the local schoolyard, I carried a few Scripture verse cards along with prayer requests that I'd written on small index cards. I was very flexible during that time. Sometimes I reflected on the Scriptures and prayed the requests, or I prayed without reading the verses at all, or I tried to memorize a verse or passage. Sometimes I thought through a personal concern and sought the Lord's guidance. What I did each morning was usually different from the last.

On our breakfast table, I had two calendars—one with Bible verses and another one with spiritual quotations. I reflected on the calendar quotes while I was eating. Although the calendars and verse cards that I carried when I walked were randomly chosen passages, I was often amazed at their similarity and how so many spoke about a particular concern of mine. The exact same verse or spiritual truth would be repeated on several different verse cards. I felt it was God's way of confirming, comforting, convicting, guiding, or even preparing me for the unexpected.

In my car, I also carried a booklet of hymns and choruses with only the lyrics. While driving to work, I took quick glances at the words and sang songs aloud as part of my praise and worship time. I also worked on memorizing verses or read a one-minute devotional book at stoplights.

Though my morning schedule was tight, I felt as if I'd spent quality time with the Lord. I had read devotionally for fifteen minutes; I had prayed, sang hymns, and reflected on Scripture for twenty minutes while walking, ten minutes during breakfast, and fifteen minutes while driving to work.

Now that I'm teaching evenings, I have more time in the morning. I still have my regular devotions, and I read a book or Scripture verses and/or pray while I'm walking.

A few years ago, the Lord prepared me for an unexpected trial while I was having my devotions and then showed me His protective presence in a very special way. That morning I read three different passages in my Bible and verse cards that spoke of how His angels protect us. One of them was Psalm 91:11: "For he will command his angels concerning you to guard you in all your ways."

After reading those verses, I began to feel edgy and wondered if something might happen. At the time I was working for a publishing company as a book editor and had a twenty-eight mile commute. For our current project, a children's book about guardian angels, a promotional poster arrived that morning with the caption, "Angels watching over me." I joked with another editor about reading three verses on the same topic during my devotions. I again felt concerned, but as I became consumed by my busy workday, I forgot about the verses and the poster.

That night I left work late at about seven o'clock. When I reached my car, I saw that I had a flat tire. My husband was working out of town more than a hundred miles away. Our offices were located in an isolated high-crime area. Car troubles unnerve me, and I began to feel anxious and afraid.

The building guards tried to help me but couldn't get the tire off because they didn't realize the hubcap was locked onto the tire. I called a friend and asked her if she could take me home, but she couldn't. Then I called a towing service that changed the tire, but I had only a small spare. The man who changed the tire advised me that it would be unsafe to drive such a long distance over freeways on the small tire. He and the security guards didn't know where I could get the flat tire repaired.

By now it was nearly nine-fifteen. Even though the verses about God's guardian angels kept coming to my mind, and I knew the Lord was attempting to comfort me, I was really beginning to panic. I finally thought of another friend who lived nearby and called him to see if he knew of any place where I could get the tire repaired. He came to work and led me to a gas station. By then it was a quarter to ten, and the station closed at ten.

Fortunately, they were able to repair the tire, and I safely made it home exhausted but grateful that God had sent His angels of mercy to help me and watch over me. Though the flat tire turned out to be a lengthy ordeal and the Lord knows how much car trouble terrifies me, He took care of me through it all. He graciously reminded me of how He'd prepared me during my devotions for that trial and kept His promise to protect me. I also realized how much I needed to trust Him more in difficult and scary situations.

Maintaining a Daily Devotional Plan

Throughout the day I try to be sensitive and aware of what God might have me do and to whom He might have me minister. My latest spiritual disciplines include practicing His presence and responding to what He desires of me at the present moment. But I'm finding those disciplines difficult to follow. As the day wears on, I become more consumed with my normal duties.

One way to keep in touch with our Lord throughout the day is to pray while driving to and from work, going to appointments, or doing regular errands. I pray silently, or if I'm struggling to overcome an ungodly thought or serious concern, I pray aloud. Sometimes I listen to Christian radio programs or cassette tapes of music or a series of messages.

Singing choruses with your children, playing story or music cassettes, or playing simple Bible games in the car is another way to have devotions with children. You can play Guess Who. Who killed the giant using a slingshot? What was the giant's name?

The women from the devotional classes that I have taught contributed the following suggestions. Place verse cards on or near your bathroom mirror, above the kitchen sink, or on your nightstand. Take a few moments to reflect on the meaning of the verses or practice learning them. Change the cards regularly. Put your children's memory verses in recipe holders on the kitchen table. Work on the verses together during mealtimes. When you know of a special concern on a particular day, such as someone having major surgery or another critical need, write the person's name on self-sticking notes and place them in strategic places to remind you to pray throughout the day.

My own devotional plan also includes regularly attending church services and meeting weekly with different Christian friends for accountability, confession, and prayer. I've also attended weekly Bible studies or small prayer-support groups or taught classes that strengthened my faith.

Having informal times of fellowship, eating a snack or meal, playing sports, or doing fun activities with Christians are other ways we can be spiritually refreshed. Even when we're sharing informally, we discover common needs and struggles. We find greater hope for our own lives when we hear how God has guided others, or we realize we're not alone in our troubles when others share their heartaches.

A couple of years ago, several people were invited to a friend's home after church for an evening snack and fellowship. One of the women spoke with me about the struggle she was having living three thousand miles away from her children and grandchildren. She spoke of her sense of loss over missing the birth of grandbabies and watching them grow. She said, "We're going to move back home, but it will take a miracle to sell our mobile home. Some people have walked away and left their homes, but we can't afford to do that." With tears in her eyes, she said, "I don't think I can stand it much longer."

As she shared her pain, I felt my own grief over wanting to sell our home and move out of a crime-ridden area. We wanted to move from the chaotic jungle of concrete cities to be near our sons and their families in a quieter country area. More than that, Ron's health was failing due to the danger and stress he constantly encountered during his congested freeway commute to Los Angeles and while calling on automotive stores and warehouses. After Ron's heart surgery eight years ago, his doctors continually urged him to make a job change.

Even though we had made every effort to make that change, God had soundly closed the door more than once. I'd felt a similar desperate concern over Ron's need for relief from his job and the terrible feeling of being trapped in a place that I not only disliked but feared. As my friend expressed her pain over not being able to adjust to God's "no," I didn't feel so alone.

Our exchange helped me identify some of my own feelings, gave me the desire to overcome my discouragement, and helped me seek the Lord's grace to accept my own situation. I realized that my attitude was the only thing I could change about our situation. That is only one example of the many divine encounters I've had and of the many ways the Lord has spoken to me and assisted me in my spiritual journey.

We rejoiced and celebrated with the couple when they were able to move back to their hometown. A couple of years later we were finally able to move, though we experienced many delays and disappointments. Even so, the Lord continued to minister to me in special and surprising ways during that difficult and lengthy process.

When we develop a devotional plan that becomes a habit and a daily lifestyle, the Lord will show Himself to us in numerous and precious ways. Our heartaches may continue, ongoing problems may remain unchanged, but our unchangeable God is always near us throughout each day to comfort and strengthen us to endure every difficult circumstance.

SUGGESTED READING

Bridges, Jerry. *The Practice of Godliness*. Colorado Springs: NavPress, 1983.

___. *The Pursuit of Holiness*. Colorado Springs: NavPress, 1978.

Chambers, Oswald. *My Utmost for His Highest*. New York: Dodd, Mead & Company, 1956.

Chambers, Oswald. *My Utmost for His Highest: An Updated Edition in Today's Language*. Grand Rapids: Discovery House Publishers, 1992.

___. *Still Higher for His Highest*. Fort Washington, Pa: Christian Literature Crusade, 1970.

Cowman, Mrs. Charles E. *Streams in the Desert,* vol. 1. Grand Rapids: Zondervan Publishing House, 1925.

Foster, Richard J. *Celebration of Discipline: The Path to Spiritual Growth*. San Francisco: Harper & Row, Publishers, 1978.

___. *Freedom of Simplicity*. San Francisco: Harper & Row, Publishers, 1981.

___. *Prayer: Finding the Heart's True Home*. San Francisco: Harper San Francisco, 1992.

Job, Rueben P., and Shawchuck, Norman. *A Guide to Prayer for All God's People*. Nashville: Upper Room Books, 1990.

___. *A Guide to Prayer for Ministers and Other Servants*. Nashville: Upper Room Books, 1983.

The One-Year Bible: New International Version. Wheaton: Tyndale House Publishers, Inc., 1986.

Lawrence, Brother. *The Practice of the Presence of God*. White Plains: Peter Pauper Press, Inc., 1963.

Spurgeon, C. H. *Spurgeon's Devotional Bible*. Grand Rapids: Baker Book House, 1964.

Stanley, Charles. *A Touch of His Peace*. Grand Rapids: Zondervan Publishing House, 1993. This is one of a series of devotional books.

Swindoll, Charles R. *Come Before Winter: And Share My Hope*. Portland: Multnomah Press, 1985. This is one of a series of devotionals.

Thompson Chain-Reference Bible, New International Version. Indianapolis: B. B. Kirkbride Bible Co., Inc., and Grand Rapids: Zondervan, 1983.

Scripture Reading: Romans 1:8-15

Practicing the Spiritual Life

How to make a devotional plan is not mentioned in Scripture, but we do see how other people made plans regarding their spiritual lives. How did Paul make his plans, and why did he desire to go to Rome?

_____

_____

_____

Too often we view ministers and missionaries as the only ones called to full-time Christian service. The Lord, however, has called each one of us to fully serve Him daily. Ask the Lord to guide you in making a devotional plan. Then write down the steps you'll take to follow it this week.

_____

_____

_____

Prayer

Many are the plans of my heart, O Lord, but it is Your purpose that prevails. Please direct my steps. How can I possibly understand my own way? All of my ways seem right to me, but, Lord, You weigh my heart; You know my plans before I even make them. I will seek Your face with all my heart; be gracious to me according to Your promise. I will consider my ways and turn my steps to Your statutes. Now show me the plans You have for me to strengthen my relationship with You. (Prov. 19:21; 20:24; 21:2; Ps. 119:58-59 paraphrased)

Prayers, Praises, and Personal Notes

_____

_____

_____

Scripture Reading: Romans 15:30-33

Practicing the Spiritual Life

Paul interceded for the people, but he also asked for their prayers. What did he ask the people to pray for?

_____

_____

_____

Faithfully interceding with another person or a small group is an important part of our devotional plan. If you're not praying with a group or a person, ask the Lord to show you whom you can pray with. If you are praying with someone, list your prayer partner's needs and intercede for him or her.

_____

_____

_____

Prayer

Jesus, as I join together with others for prayer and supplication, may we be of one accord. For You said more than once that if two of us shall agree on earth as touching anything that we shall ask, it shall be done for us by our Father in heaven. For where two or three of us are gathered together in Your name, You are there in the midst of us. O holy Intercessor, answer our prayers, because we trust in You. (Acts 1:14a RSV and KJV; Matt. 18:19-20 RSV and KJV; 1 Chron. 5:20b paraphrased)

Prayers, Praises, and Personal Notes

_____

_____

_____

_____

Scripture Reading: Proverbs 16:1-9

Practicing the Spiritual Life

What does Proverbs say about human plans and ways—in contrast to the Lord's?

_____

_____

_____

How can we apply the spiritual principles in these proverbs to our plans for our own devotional life?

_____

_____

_____

Prayer

There is no wisdom, no insight, no plan that can succeed against You, Lord. May I always remember that the plans of the righteous are just, but the advice of the wicked is deceitful. Deliver me from the woes of being an obstinate child so that I will not carry out plans that are not Yours, forming an alliance, but not by Your Spirit, heaping sin upon sin. If I plot evil, I will go astray. If I plan what is good, I will find love and faithfulness. Deal with me, Your servant, according to Your love, and teach me Your decrees, plans, and ways. (Prov. 21:30; Isa. 30:1; Prov. 12:5; 14:22; Ps. 119:125 paraphrased)

Prayers, Praises, and Personal Notes

_____

_____

_____

_____

_____

Scripture Reading: Isaiah 46:9-11

Practicing the Spiritual Life

In order to remain spiritually strong, we need the constant assurance of knowing that what God plans He accomplishes. What does God ask us to remember about Him and His purposes?

_____

_____

_____

God's plans for our life may be far different from ours. Are there any plans of your own that you need to let go of in order to accept His plans?

_____

_____

_____

Prayer

Creator of all, from one man You made every nation of people, that they should inhabit the whole earth, and You planned the times set for them and the exact places where they should live. You did this so I would seek You and reach out for You and find You, though You are not far from me. For it is in You, Sovereign Lord, that I live and move and have my being. Many are the wonders You have done. The things You planned for me—I cannot begin to recount them all to You; were I to speak and tell of them, they would be too many to declare. (Acts 17:26-28a; Ps. 40:5 paraphrased)

Prayers, Praises, and Personal Notes

_____

_____

_____

_____

Scripture Reading: Jeremiah 29:11-13

Practicing the Spiritual Life

What does God promise regarding His thoughts and plans for His people? What does the Lord require of us for His plans to be accomplished? What does He promise to do in return?

_____

_____

_____

Ask the Lord to show you His plan in a specific area of your life.

_____

_____

_____

Prayer

"O God, you are my God, earnestly I seek you; my soul thirsts for you, my body longs for you, in a dry and weary land where there is no water." Now I am looking to You and Your strength. I will seek Your face always. I will seek You, Lord, while You may be found; I will call on You while You are near. Your thoughts are precious to me, O God! How vast is the sum of them! Were I to count Your thoughts and plans for me, they would outnumber the grains of sand. (Ps. 63:1 not paraphrased; Ps. 105:4; Isa. 55:6; Ps. 139:17-18a paraphrased)

Prayers, Praises, and Personal Notes

_____

_____

_____

_____

_____

Scripture Reading: Job 42:1-6

Practicing the Spiritual Life

Even when we're faithful in our walk with the Lord, we may suffer many heartaches. Job was a godly man who lost everything precious to him. Before he lost everything, Job believed God would always bless him and cause him to prosper because he was faithful. In the end, what conclusion did Job come to about God's plans and ways? What did Job realize?

_____

_____

_____

One of the reasons we have devotions is to remain spiritually strong in trials. In what concerns or trials do you need to see God's caring presence?

_____

_____

_____

Prayer

"My days have passed, my plans are shattered, and so are the desires of my heart." "Do not withhold your mercy from me, O Lord; may your love and your truth always protect me. For troubles without number surround me; my sins have overtaken me, and I cannot see." "Be pleased, O Lord, to save me; O Lord, come quickly to help me." For I am still confident of this: I will see Your goodness in the land of the living. (Job 17:11; Ps. 40:11-12a, 13 not paraphrased; Ps. 27:13 paraphrased)

Prayers, Praises, and Personal Notes

_____

_____

_____

Scripture Reading: 2 Chronicles 29:1-3; 30:1-9

Practicing the Spiritual Life

An important part of planning our devotional life includes consistent worship and service in God's house with His people. In Hezekiah's letter to the people, what appeals and warnings did he give regarding Israel's need to return to the Lord?

_____

_____

_____

What especially spoke to you in Hezekiah's call to the people? Write a prayer of commitment to worship the Lord faithfully.

_____

_____

_____

Prayer

I love the house where You live, O Lord, the place where Your glory dwells. One thing I ask of You, this is what I seek: that I may dwell in Your house all the days of my life, to gaze upon Your beauty and to seek You in the place where I worship You. "I have seen you in the sanctuary and beheld your power and your glory. Because your love is better than life, my lips will glorify you. I will praise you as long as I live, and in your name I will lift up my hands. My soul will be satisfied as with the richest of foods; with singing lips my mouth will praise you." (Ps. 26:8; 27:4 paraphrased; Ps. 63:2-5 not paraphrased)

Prayers, Praises, and Personal Notes

_____

_____

_____

Put Your Spiritual Journey in a Devotional Journal

*"Let love and faithfulness
never leave you; bind them
around your neck, write them
on the tablet of your heart."*

PROVERBS 3:3

The way we flower into godly people is similar to the way roses grow. We can see that growth in our spiritual lives if we keep a devotional journal. As we read back over our writings, we may see when the roses blossomed as God displayed His lovely grace in our lives.

We may also see that during trials our peace wilted like rose petals in the scorching heat. Our hope was turned to dry, dead pods as heartaches worsened. Our faith was clipped and pruned until nothing remained but thorny sticks in the hardened earth. Then when that desolate season finally ended, we may again see in our journal fresh, green shoots of faith and rosebuds of hope and peace springing forth.

A journal is not only a record of our spiritual growth; it is a road map and traveler's logbook that show where we are on our journey and where we're headed. It's a recording of where we've wandered, the starting and stopping places, the scenery along the route, and how far we've traveled.

A journal is similar to a diary. It's meant to be a private experience—one for us to record our struggles and insights about our personal and spiritual life. It's not written to impress someone else; it's written for ourselves and for God alone.

Though a devotional journal helps us discover more about ourselves, this is not the main focus. Our purpose is to find out more about God and what He desires of us. "If a journal answers just one question, it is: What is God doing in my life?"[1]

Throughout the year, I reflect on Scriptures or thoughts from devotional books and then respond in my journal. By listening to Scriptures, waiting for the Lord to impress His desires on my mind, and recording my responses on paper, I begin to see how the Lord is directing me. My thoughts remain more tuned to His still, small voice when I read the Bible or other Christian books and devotionals, while at the same time writing and seeking His guidance.

Writing in a journal helps me concentrate on personal and spiritual needs, clarify my concerns, and discover a clearer sense of direction. I also have a record that I can read again. But when I don't write at all, I almost immediately forget what the Spirit of God might be impressing upon me during my reading and in prayer.

Journal writing is valuable for developing our spiritual life, but it doesn't need to be an obligation. I don't write in my journal every day. I write when I feel inspired or have gained a special insight. I write when I need to express my feelings about certain issues that I am working through. I write when I'm experiencing difficult trials and don't know what to do. I write when problems grow worse and no solution seems near.

My journal is especially comforting in times of grief and heartache. Expressing my cares, fears, and worries on paper helps me identify my concerns. I search for verses and ask God to give me comfort, direction, and support through the Word. I seek the Lord's wisdom or spiritual principles that I can apply to painful situations.

If I only wrote about my trials, then I would remain in bondage to them. By writing my concerns and requests along with Scripture, hymns, or quotes from other books that speak to those concerns, I gain spiritual balance. I receive God's healing encouragement through His Word, which helps me release the pain, gain perspective, and put the situation into His hands.

At the end of the year I usually read over my journal. Then I record in the margins how God has answered prayer or helped resolve the problem. Often I wonder why I was so anxious about different problems. God brought me through them and, compared to other trials that I'd faced, they now seem insignificant. Other times I'm reminded of long-term prayer requests that I still long for God to answer. Even so, my journals are a reminder to me of God's faithfulness.

Rueben P. Job wrote, "I have often been surprised at how I have been helped and healed by putting in writing my thoughts, prayers, questions, and responses to life. I have been even more surprised to find God's message for me in what I had written a month, year, or ten years earlier."[2]

I tend to fill my journal with requests or answers to prayer that are too quickly forgotten. As a result of our pastor's suggestion, I started recording answered prayers in a blank book. Through this experience I'm learning more about prayer, both the joyous surprises and the unexpected disappointments. I've written down what appeared to be final answers, only to have them turn into shocking reversals. Even so, recording answered prayers has strengthened my faith. Some answers have been small, others great—from giving my husband and me strength to complete difficult work projects, to providing me with a new teaching job in the town we moved to and starting a ministry that I'd desired for a long time.

A Guide for Journal Writing

I use a blank book or small loose-leaf notebook for my journals. You may prefer to do your journaling on a computer or typewriter. You may enjoy drawing pictures or sketches in your journal, making brief notes of their meaning to you. You don't need to be an artist; your pictures may be as simple as a child's stick drawings. You may also enjoy doing calligraphy to record Scriptures, prayers, or spiritual insights. If you don't feel comfortable writing, recording your journal on a cassette tape may be helpful. The tapes can be replayed during the year as desired.

Here are some suggestions to help you begin your journal. When you start an entry, record the time, day, and date at the top of the page. After you finish an entry, you may want to add a title that summarizes your thoughts or concerns. Later when you want to reread a particular entry, the title helps you locate it, and the date helps you relate that time to the sequence of events or concerns you had during that period.

You don't need to be anxious about how much you write. You may write very little while others fill volumes. You don't have to meet the standards of another person's critical eye. You're not writing for publication, so don't be concerned about grammar, punctuation, and spelling. Write without censoring thoughts. Don't allow your inner critic to shame you or cause you to feel embarrassed.

If your thoughts wander off or you become distracted by necessary obligations, write them down. If all you can think about is what you need to accomplish, stop and make a to-do list. Then set it aside and determine to concentrate on your time with the Lord.

The following guide to keeping a devotional journal may help you with your own. First, while you're reading and writing your responses, always try to bring your thought life into a balanced, godly perspective by seeking God's views. Record verses or quotes from books or tapes that especially convict or minister to you. When you need to find a certain subject, a Bible index or concordance is a valuable help. I use *Strong's Exhaustive Concordance of the Bible* and the *New International Version* of the *Thompson Chain-Reference Bible*.

This Bible has a lengthy concordance, brief analyses of each book, and an index of chain topics that includes many complete verses.

When writing Scripture passages or quotes from other books, it helps to include the chapter and verses and/or the author and title. Write a statement about why the verses or quotes spoke to you. Tell what was happening, what you were concerned about, and how your particular need was met by the passage.

Later, when I read over my writings, I've usually forgotten about that time. It seems so different in light of where my life may be months or even years afterward. I may wonder why I was so worried or may feel grateful that God graciously brought me through such a painful time.

Second, write about what is happening in your life and the concerns you have. Ask questions about how to deal with the person, problem, or situation that you're troubled about while seeking answers from the Lord.

However, "journaling does not satisfy all our queries. We may leave our journals filled with unanswered questions—Can we? Will we? When will God . . . ? A lack of closure prods us to continue the listening awareness. . . . After days or weeks or months, we are prepared to hear fragments of answers that emerge in the encouragement of a friend or the confrontation of a co-worker. In the meantime, we have learned to rest and listen even though life is full of ferment."[3]

Third, be honest with yourself and transparent. Express your true feelings, your anger, anxiety, fears, and grief. Write your frustrations, irritations, and even the struggles that may seem trivial. Recording your inner conflicts puts a name to them and frees you to address the real issues.

Write to clarify thoughts and sort through feelings. Write freely as ideas come and without thinking about what you're saying. This is an excellent way to gain insights to your true self, insights you may feel uncomfortable with or even dislike. You'll see yourself in ways you never have before when you're willing to be transparent.

In the Psalms, "David's hard honesty reveals that journaling is a place to be our true selves and to offer our true, sometimes unflattering views. . . . David moved from revenge to hopelessness to praise."[4]

Fourth, confess and repent so that the Lord may change and transform you. You don't need to be afraid to ask the Lord what He desires to reveal to you about your real self. How can you receive God's transforming love if you reject yourself? If you reject God's convicting love, how can you be changed into His likeness?

Ask the Lord to help you have His thoughts, and ask for deliverance from angry, bitter, distorted, unbalanced, and/or prejudicial attitudes. Ask Him for help in taking responsibility for your contribution to your problems or broken relationships. How and where do you need to change? Rather than rejecting yourself because you may feel ashamed, inferior, or unworthy about what you see in yourself, be open to what God is trying to show you. On the other hand, pride and self-delusion may keep you from facing the truth about yourself.

Next confess your sins in a written prayer. When you see your sins in ink, they become real; you cannot think or wish them away. As an act of cleansing and repentance, make a covenant to turn away from those wrongs, and try to make restitution where possible.

If you have any painful secrets, it also helps to write about them. They may be secrets about yourself or others, and carrying them alone has been a burden. If you're writing about personal sins or secrets, search for Scriptures to help you work through the process of finding forgiveness, healing, and personal and spiritual restoration. The Holy Spirit and Scripture are powerful; they help us overcome sin, release us from shame, and provide the support we need to change and grow.

Make a ceremony of tearing up or even burning your written confessions to help free you from the bondage of guilt and to remind you that the Lord bore all your sins and burdens on the cross. You don't have to bear them anymore. Then commit yourself to be accountable to God and another trustworthy Christian. If you feel the Lord prompting you to do so, confess to that person or a Christian counselor or pastor. Spoken confession brings darkness into the light, prevents it from remaining hidden, and helps break the power it has over us.

Above all, remember that "the Lord is gracious and compassionate, slow to anger and rich in love. The Lord is good to all; he has compassion on all he has made" (Ps. 145:8-9).

Though it's humbling and difficult, I've gone through this journaling and confession process many times and found healing, restoration, and new growth. One experience particularly changed my life. Through the Holy Spirit's conviction, I realized that I was constantly complaining to others just as the Israelites murmured bitterly against Moses and God during their many trials traveling through the desert.

I came to realize that I wasn't trusting my Lord during tough times due to my own complaining. These passages especially convicted me: "Now the people complained about their hardships in the hearing of the Lord, and when he heard them his anger was aroused." "The Lord said to Moses, 'How long will these people treat me with contempt? How long will they refuse to believe in me, in spite of all the miraculous signs I have performed among them?'" (Num. 11:1; 14:11).

I recognized that though our life was filled with many trials, God expected me to trust Him no matter what went wrong. My grumbling was only making me more anxious and afraid. I needed to change my attitude and express my trust in God. I needed to be grateful for all the wondrous ways He had led us, answered our heart cries, and performed miracles.

I still pour out my grief and heartaches to the Lord in my journal; He desires that we do so. But to gain a spiritual perspective, I write Scripture passages, prayers, and praises that affirm His abiding presence and faithfulness in all circumstances.

Finally, offer praises and express your gratitude in your journal for the specific things the Lord has accomplished. Worship God simply for who He is. Your spirit will be lifted and your heart encouraged when you rejoice in the Lord's goodness, grace, and kindness.

Be encouraged when you read over your journals again, because you'll see what the Lord is accomplishing in your life. You'll see positive spiritual growth and maturity. You'll be drawn closer and closer to our Lord and see Him in ways you never have before. And your spiritual life will become a rosebud that unfurls its petals, releases a lovely fragrance, and comes to full bloom.

Scripture Reading: Proverbs 7:1-3

Practicing the Spiritual Life

Writing about our spiritual journey in a devotional journal is not mentioned in Scripture, but the Bible is filled with the earthly concerns of God's people. According to the Proverbs passage, where are we to write God's Word?

One way to impress God's Word on your heart is to write verses that especially speak to you and to explain why they do. Start a devotional journal of your own using a small notebook, blank book, or cassette recorder. Record your concerns and a verse or passage that speaks to that need.

Prayer

Lord, open my eyes that I may see wonderful things in Your law. Teach me Your ways so that I may walk in Your paths. Put Your laws on my mind and write them on my heart. Lord, I will apply my heart to what I observe and learn a lesson from what I see. I will apply my heart to instruction and my ears to words of knowledge. (Ps. 119:18; Isa. 2:3b; Heb. 8:10b; Prov. 24:32; 23:12 paraphrased)

Prayers, Praises, and Personal Notes

Scripture Reading: Matthew 4:1-11

Practicing the Spiritual Life

Jesus kept repeating the words "It is written . . . " to quote Scripture to Satan as a means of withstanding temptation. What did Jesus say to refute Satan's claims?

_____

_____

_____

When we're struggling with sinful thoughts or actions, we can quote Scripture aloud and write it in our devotional journal to help us overcome temptation. Note any of the verses in today's passage that may help you overcome sin in your life.

_____

_____

_____

Prayer

Jesus, teach me how to watch and pray so that I will not fall into temptation. My spirit is willing, but my flesh is weak. Lead me not into temptation, but deliver me from the evil one. For no temptation has overtaken or seized me except that which is common to all people. And, God, You are faithful: You will not let me be tempted beyond my strength, but with the temptation will also provide the way to escape, that I may be able to stand up under it and endure it. Now direct my steps according to Your Word, and let no sin rule over me. (Matt. 26:41; 6:13; 1 Cor. 10:13 RSV; Ps. 119:133 paraphrased)

Prayers, Praises, and Personal Notes

_____

_____

_____

Scripture Reading: Romans 15:1-6

Practicing the Spiritual Life
What are some of the reasons Scripture was written—according to the above passage?

_____

_____

_____

Writing our concerns in a devotional journal along with Scripture helps us endure and increases our hope. Ask the Lord to teach and encourage you from the Scripture as you read and record your responses.

_____

_____

_____

Prayer
Do good to Your servant, O Lord, and give me encouragement from Your Word; teach me knowledge and good judgment, for I believe in Your commands. Teach me to be temperate, sensible, self-controlled; and sound in faith, in love, and in steadfastness and endurance. God of hope, fill me with all joy and peace as I trust in You so that I may overflow with hope by the power of the Holy Spirit. (Ps. 119:65-66; Titus 2:2 AMP; Rom. 15:13 paraphrased)

Prayers, Praises, and Personal Notes

_____

_____

_____

_____

_____

Scripture Reading: Luke 1:1-4

Practicing the Spiritual Life
What did Luke base his writings on, and why did he write this book of the Bible?

_____

_____

_____

Our faith is strengthened when we write the reasons why verses speak to our needs. Note some ways God has given you more certainty of faith from Scripture.

_____

_____

_____

Prayer
Lord, I know that faith is the assurance, the confirmation of the things I hope for, the proof of things I cannot see, and the conviction of their reality. For by the faith and trust born of faith, Your servants of old had divine testimony borne to them by Your written and spoken Word and thus obtained a good report. In the same way strengthen me to fully believe the truth that was written long ago, standing in it steadfast and firm, strong in You, Lord, with the certainty of the good news that You died for me, and never shifting from trusting You to save me. (Heb. 11:1-2; Col. 1:23a AMP paraphrased)

Prayers, Praises, and Personal Notes

_____

_____

_____

_____

Scripture Reading: 1 John 2:1-14

Practicing the Spiritual Life

What are some of the reasons John wrote to his children in the Lord and his friends?

_____

_____

_____

Writing our needs along with promises or verses that challenge us to change helps us to clarify God's desires for us and assures us of His care. Based on the above passage, write your own concerns about your spiritual life and about those you love.

_____

_____

_____

Prayer

Holy Spirit, strengthen me to prepare my mind for action, to be self-controlled, to set my hope fully on the grace that will be given to me when You, Jesus Christ, are revealed. Help me to be Your obedient child; deliver me from conforming to the evil desires I have now and to the ones I had when I lived in ignorance. But just as You who called me are holy, so I will be holy in all I do; for it is written: "Be holy, because You, Almighty God, are holy." (1 Peter 1:13-15 paraphrased)

Prayers, Praises, and Personal Notes

_____

_____

_____

Scripture Reading: 1 John 2:18-27

Practicing the Spiritual Life

What are some of the warnings John wrote about being deceived?

_____

_____

_____

We need to be careful that we're not self-deceived in believing that our own writing is from God and, therefore, infallible. No matter how inspired we may feel about what we write, we always need to be open to the Lord's correction and clarification regarding His truth. In what ways did this passage speak to you about knowing the truth?

_____

_____

_____

Prayer

Teach me Your ways, Lord, and I will walk in Your truth; give me an undivided heart that I may fear Your name. Test me, O Lord, and try me; examine my heart and my mind, for Your love is ever before me; teach me how to walk continually in Your truth. (Ps. 86:11; 26:2 paraphrased)

Prayers, Praises, and Personal Notes

_____

_____

_____

_____

_____

_____

Scripture Reading: 2 John 1:1-6

Practicing the Spiritual Life
Why did John write this brief epistle?

_____

_____

_____

Write a love letter to the Lord, asking Him to give you the grace to love others as He loves you.

_____

_____

_____

Prayer
Ever-loving Savior, this is how I know what love is: You laid down Your life for me. And I ought to lay down my life for others. And if I have any of this world's goods, material possessions, and resources for sustaining life and see my fellow believers in need and yet close my heart of compassion against them, how can Your love live and remain in me? As Your dear child, I will not love others merely in theory or in my speech, but in deeds and in truth—in practice and in sincerity. And I will follow this command; I will believe in Your name, Jesus, and I will love others as You commanded me to love them. (1 John 3:16-18 AMP, 23 paraphrased)

Prayers, Praises, and Personal Notes

_____

_____

_____

_____

PART TWO

Developing the Disciplined Life

WEEK SIX

Practice the Spiritual Disciplines

*"Buy the truth
and do not sell it;
get wisdom, discipline
and understanding."*

PROVERBS 23:23

nless a kernel of wheat falls to the ground and dies, it remains only a single seed. But if it dies, it produces many seeds. The man who loves his life will lose it, while the man who hates his life in this world will keep it for eternal life' " (John 12:23-25).

Just as a kernel of wheat must die to grow into mature stalks of grain, so must we die to the old self. When wheat is harvested, it's threshed to separate the seed from the straw. Some seeds are saved to be replanted; other seeds are crushed and ground into flour. And so it is with our personal and spiritual lives. The wheat-growing cycle illustrates the disciplining process that brings about strength of faith and spiritual maturity. But submitting to this process means discipline, and discipline means dying to self, and dying to self means new growth.

The Holy Spirit nurtures tiny seeds of spiritual trust in our minds and hearts, tenderly cultivating the fertile earth until sprouts of faith grow into mature stalks. Then He threshes and sifts our lives to separate seeds of faith from straws of mistrust.

Enduring this often-hard sifting process makes spiritual maturity possible. But we have no desire to "endure hardship as discipline" (Heb. 12:7a). We long for easy, peaceful, simple lives free of trials. We desire the blessings but not the burdens. We long for freedom to live as we please, the freedom to be what we want to be, the freedom to have it our way, the freedom to have our many desires met.

And yet "we have not advanced very far in our spiritual lives if we have not encountered the basic paradox of freedom, to the effect that we are most free when we are bound. . . . The one who would like to be an athlete, but who is unwilling to discipline his [or her] body by regular exercise and by abstinence, is not free to excel on the field or the track. . . . With one concerted voice the giants of the devotional life apply the same principle to the whole of life with the dictum: *Discipline is the price of freedom*."[1]

"Commitment means responsibility, and responsibility sounds confining.

For example, it is common in our day to define freedom as the complete absence of restraint. . . . Absolute freedom is absolute nonsense! We gain freedom in anything through commitment, discipline, and fixed habit."[2] And fixed spiritual habits are developed by self-discipline.

Setting Personal Goals and Spiritual Disciplines

Discipline then is the way to true freedom. One way to begin the committed life is to set personal goals and practice spiritual disciplines. Though we've already explored how to make plans for daily devotions, we also need to consider setting monthly, yearly, and/or lifelong goals and develop disciplines that eventually become fixed habits.

I set goals for the upcoming year during the week between Christmas and New Year's. This can also be done any time one feels the need or at specific times such as the beginning of each month or at a birthday or spiritual anniversary or at a retreat or on a vacation.

During the week after Christmas (which may stretch into two or three weeks), I seek God's guidance and select one or two Bible passages as guiding verses for the upcoming year. I ask the Lord to impress the Scripture He desires upon my heart. Sometimes I also choose a hymn for the year. The passages and hymns do not outline my spiritual goals but what God might want of me. The passages, many of which I would not have chosen for myself, are ones that God seems to impress upon my mind and heart. Most of the passages call me to a more committed walk with my Lord.

Over a period of about a week during my quiet time, I read Scripture and pray about my personal and spiritual goals. I also record my thoughts and concerns in my devotional journal along with verses and quotes from books that particularly speak to me. When I begin to feel impressed that God is leading me in a certain way, I read over my journal again. As I try to gain a clearer sense of how God is speaking to me, I find that the verses and quotes in my journal provide a foundation and a sense of direction.

Next I write my personal goals and spiritual disciplines that will help me achieve them out on index cards. At the top of each card, I write the current date and the year I plan to start. Then I write down corresponding Scripture passages or quotes from other books. I keep those disciplines simple, but they're not always easy to attain. This year I carried over the spiritual disciplines and personal goals from the previous year.

My spiritual disciplines have included having a consistent quiet time, setting dates for a devotional retreat, overcoming destructive attitudes or sins, reading a particular devotional book, or spending a longer period of time with the Lord.

Some examples of personal goals have been to lose weight, spend time with certain people, start and complete specific projects, watch less television, and refrain from buying books, clothes, or other desired items for a period of time.

I keep my spiritual and personal goals in my devotional journal. Periodically, I refer to them to help remind me of my commitment. I also make new goals throughout the year when I feel the need for greater discipline in certain areas of my life. It's sometimes easier to attain my goals if I set them for a week or for one or two months rather than for a year.

For example, I may need to spend more time having devotions. To accomplish that goal, I put down certain objectives: Set my alarm for an earlier time and determine to get up. Have devotions before taking care of any other responsibilities. Set out work clothes and teaching materials the night before.

On or near the date I set to meet a goal, I reassess my progress. How successful have I been in exercising the discipline I've set for myself? If I haven't done what I desired to do, what new objectives do I need to set? If I'm doing fine, do I need to continue for another month or more until the discipline becomes a habit? At that time, I decide if I want to extend the period or revise my plan.

At the close of each year, I also read over the goals to see if I met them and to see how that year's Bible passage proved to be significant in my life. Sometimes it has, and other times it hasn't.

My goals to follow certain disciplines used to be several pages long. Then when I read them over at the end of the year, I'd be discouraged because I had met so few of them. One year I wrote in my journal: "I don't know what it will take to get past myself or if I ever will. I have decided to make no resolutions this year at all. I have not accomplished one goal this year or for that matter any of them over the past umpteen years."

The last phrase was an exaggeration, because I had met many goals and spiritual disciplines throughout those years. At that time I felt particularly defeated. It had been a year filled with unexpected crises, and I was suffering from a sleep deprivation disorder that I later discovered. All my energy had been drained by severe exhaustion and consumed by other serious problems and major changes. That's why flexibility in setting goals is always so necessary, since God already knows what we'll experience in the days ahead.

Though I may fail to meet my personal goals and spiritual disciplines in the year I set them, I've found that I've often accomplished them in later years. I've come to realize that even when I fail, God will eventually accomplish His desires in my life if I'm truly committed and willing to work at disciplining myself.

One of the most amazing things about seeking a Biblical passage for the year has been how prophetic a few of them have been. Nine years ago the Lord seemed to strongly impress upon my heart Lamentations 3:22-26, 30-38. The first section of verses encouraged me to trust in the Lord's great love, compassion, and goodness.

It was the second set of verses that bothered me. "Let him offer his cheek to one who would strike him, and let him be filled with disgrace. Though he brings grief, he will show compassion, so great is his unfailing love. For he does not willingly bring affliction or grief to the children of men . . . to deprive a man of justice—would not the Lord see such things?" (Lam. 3:30, 32-33, 35).

At the time I was troubled by the passage and didn't want to endure such a potentially serious problem. As it turned out, my stepmother passed away in February of that year. I hadn't expected anything from the estate or to be involved in any way, because a friend of hers claimed that she had a copy of the will, and my stepmother had given her the house.

As it turned out, when the lawyer read the final will, the friend had been left out. I was named executor, and the estate was to be divided equally among my stepmother's sisters and me. Six years before my stepmother's death, the friend had talked my stepmother into giving her the house and had an early version of the will. My stepmother changed that will shortly afterward without telling the friend, who became so angered she sued for most of the small estate.

To prevent a lengthy court battle and expensive legal fees, we finally settled with the friend. She received more than the heirs. Sadly, the sister who had taken care of my stepmother for years passed away before receiving anything.

During this time my mother-in-law had Alzheimer's disease and severe diabetes and was in a convalescent home fifteen hundred miles away. A nearby relative was guardian of her affairs. Through a divine accident we discovered that my mother-in-law's bills weren't being paid. The convalescent home hadn't received payment for six months. We had to fly to Idaho and go to court so my husband could be appointed guardian.

While dealing with those situations over the next couple of years, many times I would pray a psalm, crying with David for God's intervention and for a fair resolution. Unfortunately, in both cases that didn't happen.

It took me several years to appreciate the Lord's tender mercy in preparing my heart through the Lamentations passage for such injustices, to find the healing grace to forgive, and to let both situations rest with Him. We may not see justice here on earth, but on that great and final day "the Lord will judge the world in righteousness and the peoples with equity" (Ps. 98:9b).

On the other hand, this year's passage from Colossians has been a great encouragement to me, because a portion of it speaks about a request that has been answered after many years of prayer. I'd wanted to finish this book and teach a class again on strengthening our walk with God. I hadn't thought that it would be possible due to working full- and part-time jobs, but God in His grace enabled me to do what I'd prayed for so long.

The Spiritual Disciplines

About ten years ago, I learned about spiritual disciplines when I read Richard J. Foster's book, *Celebration of Discipline: The Path to Spiritual Growth.* I used those disciplines as a basis for my own. As part of my yearly devotional plan, I'm trying to incorporate certain spiritual disciplines in my life, though it has been a long, slow process.

It takes time, often years, to incorporate the disciplines into our daily lives. God is gracious, patient, and tender, but He desires our utmost for His highest. Yet it requires constant work to maintain the disciplines. It's easier for me to forget them than to keep them, because I become so caught up by the obligations of day-to-day living. Even though I often fail, God continues to help me strengthen my commitment to persevere in keeping the spiritual disciplines.

Here is a brief overview of some of the disciplines that we can build into our life. The devotional-life discipline is planning for and committing ourselves to regularly spend time alone with the Lord, to read Scripture and other

Christian books for our own renewal and growth. It's developing a spiritual lifestyle that we seek to daily maintain.

The worship-centered discipline is to meet regularly with other Christians for celebration, confession, praise, and prayer. Worshiping the Lord is glorifying Him for what He has done for us, what He is doing for us, and for who He is without doing anything for us at all.

Prayer is the discipline of constant intercession for those we love, those in need of salvation and spiritual renewal, and for ministers, missionaries, and other servants of the Lord. This also includes personal confession, intercession, and thanksgiving to our great and loving Savior.

Planting the Word in our mind and heart is the discipline of regularly learning and studying Scripture to help us live according to God's desires, to equip us to serve, and to enable us to share our faith with others.

Pursuing holiness is the discipline of confessing and overcoming personal sins, and living in a godly way. Maintaining a holy life means more than laying aside sins; it means taking up godly habits in their place. It means denying self and being crucified with Christ so that we might become more like Him.

The Spirit-controlled discipline means that we yield to the Holy Spirit's direction and guidance. The Spirit is our counselor and teacher who through the Word "guides us into all truth" (John 16:13). And He empowers us to do the will of God and live a holy life.

Practicing God's presence is the discipline of constantly speaking with the Lord throughout the day as we go about our ordinary work. It means growing in our awareness of His presence and continually worshiping and praising Him for being with us at all times.[3]

Presenting ourselves for service means seeking the Lord's guidance regarding what He would have us do at this moment. It is the discipline of serving the Lord and other people in everything we do by sharing our faith, expressing compassion, and doing practical acts of service.

Pressing on in painful circumstances is the discipline of keeping our faith when everything not only goes wrong but becomes worse. It means holding onto the Lord during deep trials and asking Him to hold onto us when we feel weak in faith and hope.

After reading the brief synopsis of the spiritual disciplines, you may feel as I often do. I'll never be able to follow them. Discipline is hard work. Leading a disciplined life or following a set routine has never been easy for me. I'd rather do as I please, and I always try to do more than I can possibly accomplish.

It's a daily struggle, because I'd prefer to have the freedom to do the things I enjoy instead of doing what the Lord desires and meeting my commitments. I am discovering, however, that freedom without discipline causes chaos. Freedom with discipline creates order.

The more disciplined I become, the more I'm able to do what Christ desires of me. And doing what the Lord wants of me is more deeply satisfying than the empty feeling of doing as I please.

I realize that only God's power can help us develop the disciplined life and that it takes a lifetime. I haven't written this devotional book as someone who has completely incorporated the disciplines into my life. I'm still traveling on this spiritual journey along life's road.

Though many Christian books and especially the spiritual classics set high standards for godliness, few of us consistently attain them. I fail miserably despite my desire to live the disciplined spiritual life. I sin daily even though I don't want to, but I do so either deliberately or without meaning to.

Even Paul said, "We know that the law is spiritual; but I am unspiritual, sold as a slave to sin. I do not understand what I do. For what I want to do, I do not do, but what I hate I do. . . . I know that nothing good lives in me, that is, in my sinful nature. For I have the desire to do what is good, but I cannot carry it out" (Rom. 7:14-15, 18).

God desires that we let go of the failures and sins of the past and the present. He longs for us to continue to pursue Him no matter how many times we fall and trip over ourselves. We are broken people, and He desires to glorify Himself through our brokenness. As paradoxical as it may seem, God is more honored by humble servants than by ones who think they're super competent and spiritually superior.

The Lord has promised His grace and the Holy Spirit's power to enable us to live in accordance with what God desires. We may repeatedly falter and fail to meet our spiritual goals, but we can keep pressing on, keep on disciplining and training ourselves, keep on strengthening our faith. By discipline we build commitment, and by commitment we build faith, and by faith we build spiritual endurance and strength.

Scripture Reading: Luke 2:36-38; 4:14-19

Practicing the Spiritual Life

The discipline of worship includes daily offering of thanksgiving and regularly attending worship services. Jesus and Anna worshiped faithfully in God's house. In what ways did they worship and serve God?

_____

_____

_____

In what ways does their example speak to you about your own worship habits and service?

_____

_____

_____

Prayer

"I rejoiced with those who said to me, 'Let us go to the house of the Lord.'"
"I will praise you, O Lord, with all my heart; I will tell of all your wonders. I will be glad and rejoice in you; I will sing praise to your name, O Most High." I sing to the glory of Your name; I offer You glory and praise. How awesome are Your deeds! Praise be to You, Lord God; let the sound of Your praises be heard. (Ps. 122:1; 9:1-2 not paraphrased; Ps. 66:2-3a, 8 paraphrased)

Prayers, Praises, and Personal Notes

_____

_____

_____

_____

_____

Scripture Reading: 1 Kings 18:20-39

Practicing the Spiritual Life

Prayer is the discipline of constant intercession for those in need of salvation and spiritual renewal. What did Elijah ask of the Lord? How did the people respond?

_____

_____

_____

Write the names of people who need to turn back to the Lord; commit your-self to pray faithfully for them.

_____

_____

_____

Prayer

"Hear my prayer, O Lord; listen to my cry for mercy. In the day of my trouble I will call to you, for you will answer me. Among the gods there is none like you, O Lord; no deeds can compare with yours. All the nations you have made will come and worship before you, O Lord; they will bring glory to your name. For you are great and do marvelous deeds; you alone are God." (Ps. 86:6-10)

Prayers, Praises, and Personal Notes

_____

_____

_____

_____

_____

Scripture Reading: Psalm 119:67-80

Practicing the Spiritual Life

Planting the Scriptures in our minds and hearts is an essential discipline for spiritual growth. What caused the psalmist to learn, obey, and delight in God's Word?

_____

_____

_____

According to the verses in Psalm 119, how can learning Scripture minister to you and help with your particular needs?

_____

_____

_____

Prayer

Gracious Father, teach me how to bind Your commands and the wisdom of Your words upon my heart and to fasten them around my neck forever. When I walk, they will guide me; when I sleep, they will watch over me; when I awake, they will speak to me. For Your commands are a lamp, and Your teaching is a light, and the corrections of discipline are the way to life. (Prov. 6:21-23 paraphrased)

Prayers, Praises, and Personal Notes

_____

_____

_____

_____

_____

Scripture Reading: Hebrews 12:1-16

Practicing the Spiritual Life

Pursuing holiness is the discipline of renouncing sins and living in a godly way. What does discipline produce in our lives?

_____

_____

_____

For what sinful habits do you need the Spirit's overcoming power? What holy habits do you need to incorporate into your life?

_____

_____

_____

Prayer

Jesus, You said that You rebuke and discipline those whom You love. For You bore my sins in Your body on the tree, so that I might die to sins and live for righteousness; by Your wounds I have been healed. Therefore, Christ, since You suffered in Your body, I will arm myself with the same attitude, because as I suffer in my body, it helps me to be done with sin. For You saved me and called me to live a holy life—not because of anything I have done, but because of Your own purpose and grace. By Your divine power, You have given me everything I need for life and godliness through my knowledge of You, Lord, who called me by Your own glory and goodness. (Rev. 3:19a; 1 Peter 2:24; 4:1; 2 Tim. 1:9a; 2 Peter 1:3 paraphrased)

Prayers, Praises, and Personal Notes

_____

_____

_____

Scripture Reading: Philippians 3:10-14

Practicing the Spiritual Life

We come to know Christ more intimately when we practice the discipline of seeking His constant presence as we go about our regular work. In what ways did Paul want to know Christ? What did Paul continue to do even though he had not reached his goal?

_____

_____

_____

Write a note or prayer of commitment asking the Lord to help you daily practice His presence.

_____

_____

_____

Prayer

Jesus, if it is Your will, it is better that I suffer for doing good than for doing evil. For You died for my sins once for all, the righteous for the unrighteous, to bring me to God. O give me a heart to know You, to know You are Lord. You have never forsaken those who seek You. For You said, "Seek My face." My heart says to You, "I will seek Your face." (1 Peter 3:17-18a; Jer. 24:7a; Ps. 9:10b; Ps. 27:8 RSV paraphrased)

Prayers, Praises, and Personal Notes

_____

_____

_____

_____

Scripture Reading: Colossians 3:23-24

Practicing the Spiritual Life

Daily presenting ourselves for service means that we constantly seek to do what the Lord desires. Though the passage was written for slaves, we can apply the principles to our lives. How are we to serve, according to these verses?

_____

_____

_____

Write some specific ways you can serve the Lord and others in ordinary duties. Make a commitment to do a special act of service.

_____

_____

_____

Prayer

Lord, You have commanded me to do good, so I will be rich in good deeds; I will be generous and willing to share. I will serve You and hold fast to You. For those who have served well gain an excellent standing and great assurance in their faith in You, Christ Jesus. (1 Tim. 6:18; Deut. 13:4b; 1 Tim. 3:13 paraphrased)

Prayers, Praises, and Personal Notes

_____

_____

_____

_____

_____

Scripture Reading: Ruth 1:19-22; 4:13-17

Practicing the Spiritual Life

Pressing on in painful circumstances is the discipline of keeping our faith when we experience devastating trials. How did Naomi feel about the loss of her husband and sons? What joy did the Lord bring to Naomi out of her great sorrow?

_____

_____

_____

In what ways did Naomi's story minister to you about keeping your faith during painful times? In what trials do you need the Lord's comforting support?

_____

_____

_____

Prayer

Sovereign God, why is light given to me when I am in misery, and life when I am bitter of soul? Why is life given to me when the way is hidden and You have hedged me in? "What I feared has come upon me; what I dreaded has happened to me. I have no peace, no quietness; I have no rest, but only turmoil." O Holy Comforter, guard me and keep me in perfect and constant peace, for my mind is stayed on You, because I commit myself to You, lean on You, and hope confidently in You. (Job 3:20, 23 paraphrased; Job 3:25-26 not paraphrased; Isa. 26:3 AMP paraphrased)

Prayers, Praises, and Personal Notes

_____

_____

_____

WEEK SEVEN

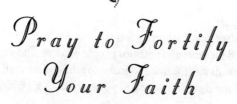

Pray to Fortify Your Faith

*"Pray in the Spirit on all
occasions with all kinds of
prayers and requests.
With this in mind, be alert
and always keep on
praying for all the saints."*

EPHESIANS 6:18

*H*ave you ever felt at a loss when you prayed about your greatest concerns or for others in difficult situations? Or maybe you talk to God as if He's your closest friend, but you still have times when you just don't know how to pray.

On the other hand, you may feel that your prayers are ineffectual. You have interceded for years and years for people you love and care about deeply, but your prayers haven't seemed to make any difference at all. You think that if you had said the right words or had possessed enough faith, then you'd see the answers you desire.

Perhaps you've felt as I have when someone shared a serious need, but your prayers seemed so inadequate in light of the gravity of the problem. A friend once wrote me a letter expressing her own fears about the unforeseen and sudden hardships they'd experienced. Their family had to move because her husband lost his job due to a change in company ownership. They couldn't support a large family on the minimum-wage jobs in the rural area where they lived. Her husband finally found a job several hundred miles away. This meant uprooting teenagers while leaving one senior-high-schooler behind. On top of all this, several family members had serious health problems.

In her letter, she expressed the fears she felt in adjusting to their new situation: "I think the thing I'm having the hardest struggle with is trying to get victory over my fear. I'm scared because of no money in the bank, no life insurance on my husband, no health insurance for the rest of us, and scared of his health and mine. Scared over my husband's job situation. Scared of our son on his own and our other son wanting to return to our hometown. Scared because I can't find a job, and juggling bills every month becomes more difficult. And what if the owner decides to sell the house? What if one of our ancient cars croaks? What if I have my devotions and feel strengthened, and the phone rings, and my heart drops, and I think: *What next?*"

After I read her letter and prayed for her family, I still felt as if my intercession for them was inadequate. I, too, often wondered, what next? And what difference would my prayers make since their difficulties seemed so enormous? After they moved again to a different area, God provided both of them with jobs and the necessary medical coverage. Even so, they wouldn't have chosen to make two moves or go through such hardships.

When we pray for the seemingly impossible, our helplessness often seems greater than our faith. We're not alone. We see times when David, Elijah, Job, Jeremiah, Naomi, Paul, and many others in the Bible felt alone, forsaken, and helpless. Their prayers and thoughts often express how we may feel and show us the many ways we may come before God.

Their prayers ranged from simple requests asked in childlike faith to the cries of the brokenhearted seeking understanding during a tragedy. Some prayers were quiet intercession offered alone in a room; others were the anguished pleas for safety of those feeling abandoned in the deserts and mountains. Scripture is also filled with joyous exclamations of celebration, praise, and worship.

According to Scripture, we can share every need with our Lord—our unspeakable sorrows and even those things we consider too trivial for His interest. One time I had a painful kidney infection, and the doctor's office was in a sprawling seven-story complex. Finding a space anywhere near the building in the parking lot the size of a football field was impossible. That day I'd asked God to give me a parking spot near the building. He gave me one in front of the bank of steps leading to the offices.

Praying Scripture

Even though God had answered many of my prayers in wonderful ways, I often felt as if my intercession was ineffective for loved ones, friends, our pastor, and missionaries in particular. When I lacked the words to intercede for myself and others, I often prayed a psalm. But it wasn't until I read a Wycliffe article, "Lord, Bless Charles" by Sarah Gudschinsky, that I discovered the principle of praying any fitting passage from God's Word for every kind of need.

Sarah said that once while she was praying for fellow missionaries on the designated day according to the prayer directory, she realized that she didn't know many of them personally. And she didn't have any recent news about them.

She wrote, "My prayer is dry and hurried and impersonal—bless the Grubers, and bless . . . Wait a minute! The next name on the list is my own.

And I wonder with shock and horror if others today are praying: 'and bless Sarah and bless Shirley . . . and . . . '—not really praying for me at all. . . . It occurs to me if I use Scripture as a base for my prayer, it may become more meaningful—more like the prayer I need from others."

In Sarah's prayers for colleagues, she started personalizing the Scripture for each person. She chose Colossians 1:9-13 to pray for Charles. Verse 11 reads, "Strengthened with all power according to his glorious might so that you may have great endurance and patience, and joyfully giving thanks to the Father."

This is a portion of her prayer from that same verse for Charles that she personalized to read:

"Strengthen him with all Thy glorious power—the power that raised Christ from the dead.

"Take his weakness and inability that it might be lost in the ocean depths of Thine own omnipotence.

"Teach him patience and long-suffering.

"Make him patient with the shortcomings and irritating habits of his co-workers in all the daily annoyances and friction. Make him patient in the multitude of interruptions to the problem that he has laid out. Give him long-suffering in the unreasonable upsets and delays that slow the work. And grant to him patience with himself, with his own faults and weaknesses."

After reading Sarah's article on prayer, I felt as if a whole new dimension of praying God's Word had opened up to me. I felt closer to the heart of how God would want me to pray for myself and others. Since then I've written many personalized Scripture prayers.

Scripture Prayer Cards and Notebooks

If you struggle with knowing how to pray and what words to use, you may find it helpful to write Scripture prayers on index cards or in a blank book or loose-leaf notebook.

Here are some suggestions on how you can record prayers of your own. Write your requests by paraphrasing Scripture so you can address God intimately from His words. Personalize the verse or passage so you can pray for your own concerns and for others. Write prayers and praises using a phrase, verse, passage, or several verses from different chapters in the Bible that speak to you or address the needs you're concerned about.

Read several different versions of the Bible; then make an amplified prayer by including additional words from those versions.

Find an appropriate verse and insert the names of loved ones, friends, or anyone you desire to pray for. For example, personalize John 3:16 by including the names of people and praying for their salvation.

Here's a personalized prayer for a particular person, using three different passages—Colossians 4:12b, Proverbs 4:26-27, and Ephesians 6:10. (I've used the name Jim as an example):

Lord, I'm constantly wrestling in prayer for Jim that he may stand firm in all the will of God, mature and fully assured. Make level paths for his feet, and may Jim take only the ways that are firm. May he not swerve to the right or the left; may he keep his feet from evil. May Jim become strong in You, Lord, and firm in Your mighty power.

When we read and search for the right passages, we begin to discover how to pray for a specific person or need. The verses help us intercede according to God's Word when we don't know what to say.

As we seek guidance, the Holy Spirit may speak to our hearts and impress upon us where we can obtain help. The Lord sometimes uses us to answer our prayers or leads us to the person who has the exact information needed to solve our problem.

But often our greatest concerns are beyond our ability to solve, and then the wisest course is to record our requests on cards or in a prayer notebook, continue to intercede using Scripture prayers, and wait upon our Sovereign Lord to answer.

Many of us have felt greatly discouraged and depressed because we've waited years without our heartfelt prayers being answered. It took me a long time to realize that the source of my discouragement was not my lack of faith but my expectations and how I presumed God should answer.

We often have definite expectations of how, when, and in what manner God should answer our prayers. Our faith may be genuine, and God is hearing our prayers, but we need to realize that the people we're praying for have absolute freedom to do and think as they please, and so do we for that matter.

Though the Holy Spirit is speaking to those we're interceding for about their spiritual needs, they're free to say, "No." Or "I'm not interested." "Not now, maybe later." Or they may simply lack interest or be bitter toward God because of a disappointment or tragedy or a hurtful experience with another

Christian or the church. Or they may be in bondage to addictive sins they're unable or unwilling to be freed from, and they don't think God could possibly accept or forgive them.

Our expectations may not be met or our prayers answered in the way we desired. Our hope and encouragement comes from having the confidence that God longs to change the hearts and transform the people we're praying for even more than we do. Jesus and the Holy Spirit are praying with us according to God's will for those we're concerned about.

The purpose of prayer is not to gain the answers we want, as holy as our requests may be; the purpose of prayer is to persevere without ceasing, to never give up, and to believe that God desires to answer. Through prayer we receive the Lord's strength, support, and tender, loving care. And we learn how to trust Him no matter what the final outcome may be.

One way we can gain the strength we need to continue praying is to write Scripture prayers. If you write more prayers than you can cover during your devotional time, intercede for certain people on Monday, other ones on Tuesday, doing the same throughout the week. Finally, be sure to note the date when your prayers have been answered, along with a few thoughts about how God guided or intervened in each situation. Remember to include prayers of rejoicing and thanksgiving next to the places where you've received answers.

Write answers to prayer in a separate notebook. Every few months read them again. You'll be surprised and blessed afresh by how God has answered. You'll be reminded of the ways God has led you safely through trials you had long forgotten about. You'll be encouraged and strengthened by His never-failing presence in your life—and you'll be adding more praises!

Scripture Reading: John 16:33–17:26

Practicing the Spiritual Life
What did Jesus ask for the disciples and for all believers?

_____

_____

_____

How did this Scripture speak to you about prayer and oneness with Christ?

_____

_____

_____

Prayer
Father God, I pray that out of Your glorious riches You may strengthen me with power through Your Spirit in my inner being, so that You, Christ Jesus, may dwell in my heart through faith and that I may be one with You and remain in You. And I pray that I will be rooted and established in love and may have power, together with all the saints, to grasp how wide and long and high and deep Your love for me is, Christ Jesus, and to know this love that surpasses knowledge—that I may be filled to the measure of all Your fullness. You are able to do immeasurably more than all I ask or imagine, according to Your power that is at work within me. To You be glory in the church and in Christ Jesus throughout all generations, forever and ever! Amen. (Eph. 3:16-21 paraphrased)

Prayers, Praises, and Personal Notes

_____

_____

_____

_____

_____

Scripture Reading: Romans 8:22-27

Practicing the Spiritual Life
Why and how is the Holy Spirit praying for us?

_____

_____

_____

In what ways did this passage give you hope regarding your own prayer life?

_____

_____

_____

Prayer
Spirit of God, before I call, You will answer; while I am still speaking, You will hear me. Help me to build myself up in my most holy faith and to pray in Your Spirit. Holy and wise Counselor, teach me all things and remind me of everything that Jesus said. Guide me in Your truth and teach me, for You are God my Savior, and my hope is in You all day long. Humbly I ask that You will guide me in what is right and teach me Your way. (Isa. 65:24; Jude 20; John 14:26; Ps. 25:5, 9 paraphrased)

Prayers, Praises, and Personal Notes

_____

_____

_____

_____

_____

_____

Scripture Reading: Romans 8:32-34

Practicing the Spiritual Life
What did God promise believers in these verses?

_____

_____

_____

Jesus Himself is interceding for you. How can this promise help you strengthen your own prayer life?

_____

_____

_____

Prayer
I will lift up my eyes to the hills. Where does my help come from? My help comes from You, Lord, who made heaven and earth. You will not let my foot be moved; You who keep me will not slumber; indeed, You who keep Israel will neither slumber nor sleep. Lord, You are my keeper; You are my shade at my right hand. The sun will not smite me by day nor the moon by night. You will preserve me from all evil; You will preserve my soul. You will preserve my going out and my coming in from this time forth and forevermore. You are able to save me completely because I come to You, God, through Jesus, who always lives to intercede for me. (Ps. 121 KJV and RSV; Heb. 7:25 paraphrased)

Prayers, Praises, and Personal Notes

_____

_____

_____

_____

_____

Scripture Reading: Matthew 6:5-13

Practicing the Spiritual Life
What were Jesus' instructions regarding prayer?

_____

_____

_____

How did this passage speak to you about prayer?

_____

_____

_____

Prayer
Our Father in heaven, hallowed be Your name. Blessed be Your glorious name, and may it be exalted above all blessing and praise. Your kingdom come, Your will be done on earth as it is in heaven. Teach me to do Your will, for You are my God.

Give me this day my daily bread. Teach me, Lord, to treasure the words of Your mouth more than my daily bread. I will forgive others their trespasses, and then You will also forgive my trespasses. And lead me not into temptation, but deliver me from evil. For no temptation has seized me except what is common to others. You are faithful, God; You will not let me be tempted beyond what I am able to bear. But when I am tempted, You will provide a way out so that I can stand up under it. For Yours is the kingdom, and the power, and the glory, forever. Amen. (Matt. 6:9b KJV; Neh. 9:5b AMP; Matt. 6:10 KJV; Ps. 143:10a KJV; Matt. 6:11; Job 23:12b; Matt. 6:12-13a; 1 Cor. 10:13; Matt. 6:13b KJV paraphrased)

Prayers, Praises, and Personal Notes

_____

_____

Scripture Reading: Luke 11:5-10

Practicing the Spiritual Life
How did the Lord liken prayer to a friend asking for loaves of bread?

_____

_____

_____

Some of our most urgent requests remain unanswered despite our persistence in prayer. Are you about to give up, or have you stopped praying for certain concerns, desires, and/or people? If so, ask the Lord to show you how to intercede according to His will. Then write your own Scripture prayer that includes your requests.

_____

_____

_____

Prayer
"Hear my voice when I call, O Lord; be merciful to me and answer me." "Do not hide your face from me, do not turn your servant away in anger; you have been my helper. Do not reject me or forsake me, O God my Savior." I will seek You, Lord, and You will answer me; deliver me from all my fears. I will wait patiently for You; turn to me and hear my cry. For, God, You have promised that I have this assurance in approaching You: that if I ask anything according to Your will, You hear me. And if I know that You hear me, whatsoever I ask, I know that I have the petitions that I desired of You. (Ps. 27:7, 9 not paraphrased; Ps. 34:4; 40:1; 1 John 5:14-15 KJV paraphrased)

Prayers, Praises, and Personal Notes

_____

_____

Scripture Reading: Luke 18:1-8; 1 Thessalonians 5:16-18

Practicing the Spiritual Life

How are we to pray, according to these passages?

_____

_____

_____

Record the areas in which you need the Lord's encouragement to help you keep persevering in prayer.

_____

_____

_____

Prayer

Heavenly Father, I approach Your throne of grace with confidence so that I may receive mercy and find grace to help me in my time of need. I lift up before You my requests, prayers, intercessions, and thanksgiving for every-one—for kings, presidents, and all those in authority that we may live peace-ful and quiet lives in all godliness and holiness. This is good and pleases You, God my Savior, for You want all people to be saved and to come to the knowl-edge of the truth. For this reason, I rejoice in You, Lord. I give thanks to You because of Your righteousness, and I sing praises to Your name, O Lord Most High. (Heb. 4:16; 1 Tim. 2:1-4; Phil. 3:1; Ps. 7:17 paraphrased)

Prayers, Praises, and Personal Notes

_____

_____

_____

_____

Scripture Reading: 1 Chronicles 16:8-12; Philippians 4:4-7

Practicing the Spiritual Life

How are we to praise the Lord, and for what are we to thank Him? What will the Lord do for us after we present our requests and offer Him thanksgiving?

_____

_____

_____

Offer your own praises and thanksgiving to the Lord for what He is doing in your life and for answers to prayer.

_____

_____

_____

Prayer

Lord, with all the earth I make a joyful sound to You. I serve You with gladness! I come into Your presence with singing! I know, Lord, that You are God! It is You who made me, and I am Yours. I belong to You; I am a sheep of Your pasture. I enter Your gates with thanksgiving and Your courts with praise! I give thanks to You and bless Your name! For You are good and Your steadfast love endures forever, Your faithfulness to all generations. Praise You, Lord. Praise You for Your mighty deeds; praise You for Your exceeding greatness! (Ps. 100; 150:1a, 2 RSV paraphrased)

Prayers, Praises, and Personal Notes

_____

_____

_____

_____

WEEK EIGHT

Plant the Word in Your Mind and Heart

*"His delight is in the law of the Lord,
and on his law he meditates day and night.
He is like a tree planted by streams of water,
which yields its fruit in season
and whose leaf does not wither.
Whatever he does prospers."*

PSALM 1:2-3

*T*he human brain has many intriguing features. Whether we're awake or asleep, the information our brain sends and receives could overwhelm a telephone system. Our brain is like volumes of encyclopedias that store a wide variety of subject matter.

Our memory, however, is selective. Ron can chart the history of our married life by the cars we have owned. I couldn't tell you the make or model of the last car we had. And how many of us have memorized information for an exam and immediately forgotten it after the test was over?

This selective memory also applies to learning Scripture. A few people may be able to recall hundreds of Bible passages, while most of us retain only a few verses that we've learned. Though I've "memorized" many verses over the years, I can only recite a few of them. So why do I attempt to learn Scripture? I've found that it helps me gain a deeper understanding of the verse or the passage. As I keep repeating the verse, the meaning becomes more personal and real to me.

One of the greatest helps in memorizing is to know how we assimilate information. Everyone has a predominant learning style, such as auditory, visual, and/or tactile-kinesthetic. If you're a tactile-kinesthetic learner like me, you need to see how something is done—to feel, touch, and do things with your hands. For example, I enjoy using a computer, but I have a difficult time learning programs by reading instruction manuals. I learn the best when I can see the teacher demonstrate program procedures while I practice them at the same time.

If you're a visual learner, you gain information from reading charts, diagrams, directions, and seeing illustrations. You may see pictures or words in your mind and remember them. You may be able to picture the words of a verse on the page and learn Scripture that way.

You may be an auditory learner. You learn best by listening to a speaker or hearing music. You remember songs easier than something you read. Learning Scripture songs is a great way for auditory learners to memorize.

Everyone uses all three learning styles, but one or two are more predominant. To effectively learn Scripture, here are some methods to help auditory, visual, or tactile-kinesthetic learners. Using all of the following ways to learn a verse or passage would be too confusing. Try different ideas until you find the ones that work well for you.

Implanting the Word in the Mind and Heart

Learn Scriptures that express your own needs. When I have a particular concern or am going through a trial, learning verses that match those needs is a constant reminder of God's caring presence. Or if I'm struggling with a sin in my life, I concentrate on verses that help me work on overcoming it.

Write or type the Scripture passage on index cards. You can practice learning a verse throughout the day by making copies of the same Scripture on several cards. Put one by your bed with your devotional materials, one in your car, one where you eat your meals, and one at work. If you walk or use a stationary bicycle for exercise, you can also work on memorizing Scripture during that time.

Look for word patterns and emphasize certain words to help you memorize a verse or passage. Underline the first couple of words of each sentence and the same words in a verse. Emphasize the underlined words when you say them out loud to set the pattern in your mind. Use those words for memorization cues. If you remember the first word of a phrase or sentence, or words that are repeated, it's much easier to learn the rest of the verse.

Note the pattern of repetition in Psalm 119:16-17 and the emphasis on *I will* and *word:* "I delight in your decrees; *I will* not neglect your *word.* Do good to your servant, and *I will* live; *I will* obey your *word.*"

Memorize a phrase at a time. Say the first phrase five to ten times, emphasizing key words; repeat the first and second phrases together the same number of times. Keep adding and repeating more phrases in that manner. Finally, repeat the whole verse aloud ten times or more. You can avoid rote memorization of the verse by thinking about its meaning as you learn it.

Keep your thoughts focused on the verse. Many of us struggle with meandering thoughts. Our mind wanders from one concern or duty to the next. I sometimes hold out my hand as if it's a stop sign to help me refocus my thoughts on the verse. It may encourage you to realize that most of us have to keep disciplining our minds while we're trying to memorize a verse. Repeat the verse out loud to keep your thoughts on it. Run your finger along the words to hold your attention as you read aloud.

Write or typewrite the verse or passage several times to reinforce it in your memory. Then share the copies with someone else as an added ministry. My friend Carolyn chose Psalm 121 to learn and wrote several copies on floral stationery. Then she sent them to friends. One woman called and told me she was extremely ill and going through other difficult trials and had asked the Lord to send her encouragement. The next day she received the handwritten psalm. She felt the Lord had sent her the encouragement she had prayed for. I was also greatly comforted when Carolyn gave a copy of the psalm to me as we were facing major changes in our lives.

Meditate on the Scripture that you're learning. Charles Stanley wrote, "I have come to realize that my thirst is quenched as I spend time meditating on the Word of God. Meditation is not mystical. Rather, it is the extremely practical and nourishing exercise of pondering and thinking on what God is saying through His Word. It is the art of asking questions of the Scriptures and then of yourself and discovering how the truth examined can be applied to your life and the particular problems you face."[1]

As I meditate on the Word and seek the Lord's thoughts, He speaks to me in many ways. He comforts, convicts, and counsels me. He delivers me from sin and distorted thinking. And I continue to develop a deeper relationship with Him.

Learn Scripture songs. If you enjoy singing, one of the easiest ways to memorize is to learn Scripture choruses. I enjoy singing Scripture more than just saying it, and I remember it longer because I associate the words with music.

Take plenty of time to learn Scripture. The length of time to memorize a verse or passage isn't important. I've spent several weeks or months learning passages.

Keep reviewing the passage once you've learned it. Repeating a verse helps us retain it. If we haven't practiced the verse for a day or two, we may be able to repeat most of it if we just glance at the first few words. But once we stop going over the verse, it easily slips out of our memory banks. Still, it's much easier to relearn a passage that has been previously memorized.

Memorize Scripture to help you keep your thoughts on the Lord. A verse or a Scripture song may keep playing over and over in my mind. Sometimes I stop and ask the Lord what He's trying to say to me. Other times I realize it's His way of keeping my thoughts tuned to His presence.

Learning a Particular Passage by Heart

Here are some ways to learn Scripture using Colossians 3:15-16. "Let the peace of Christ rule in your hearts, since as members of one body you were called to peace. And be thankful. Let the word of Christ dwell in you richly as you teach and admonish one another with all wisdom, and as you sing psalms, hymns and spiritual songs with gratitude in your hearts to God."

Use hand gestures or sign language. Hand signing is a great way to reinforce a verse in your mind. Or make up your own hand gestures. For example, "Let the peace of Christ rule in your hearts." *Let* means to allow to pass, so make a gesture as if you're allowing someone to pass by. For *peace* make a peace sign. For *rule* pretend you're holding a ruler. For *hearts* draw the shape in the air or place your hand on your chest.

Associate words with mental pictures of certain things or people to learn the passage. As you repeat key words, relate the word *peace* with a dove, *Christ* with a familiar painting, *rule* with a measuring ruler, *hearts* with red hearts, *members* with people at church, and *word* with a Bible.

Do a study of key words. We learn verses easier when we understand their meaning. The passage also becomes more personal, touches our heart in a deeper way, and gives us greater insight into the richness of Scripture. Study the passage in several different versions of the Bible and in commentaries. Look up key words from the Old Testament in Hebrew using *Nelson's Expository Dictionary of the Old Testament*. For New Testament words in the Greek use *An Expository Dictionary of New Testament Words* by W. E. Vine. *Strong's Exhaustive Concordance of the Bible* has both Hebrew and Greek dictionaries.

This is what *peace* and *rule* mean in this passage. "Let the peace of God rule in your heart, since as members of one body you were called to peace." The Greek word for *peace* means quietness and rest and to set at one again; it also means to have harmonious relationships. *Rule* means to arbitrate or act as an umpire or referee.

Paraphrase the passage. Once you've studied the meaning of the words, paraphrase the verses or make up Scripture prayers as another way to deepen your understanding. For example: "May the quietness and rest that comes with peace help me to be at one with others. May peace be like an umpire that rules my heart with fairness so that I may work well with the other members of the team who are the body of Christ."

Learn the Word to help you with everyday needs and in times of stress. A while ago I discovered how a phrase from the Colossians passage helped me to reduce panic in an emergency situation. I went through a frightening experience when my throat went into spasms and restricted my air and swallowing passages. I felt as if I were being strangled and would choke to death.

During one of several reactions, I was making a frantic drive to the doctor's office. I kept praying, "Let the peace of Christ," inhaling as I said the words and then exhaling "rule in my heart." I kept repeating the phrase to calm myself and to keep my blood pressure from soaring, which it had done during the attacks.

I kept praying the verse over and over again during the following weeks as my throat continued to close up, as I went to several specialists and through the traumatic regime of numerous tests, x-rays, and even misdiagnosis. I found out that the spasms were caused by a chronic dry throat from using a breathing machine at night for a sleep disorder. Though the x-rays showed that I had nose and throat obstructions, I was grateful that the problem could be relieved without having surgery. The most comforting discovery was how repeating that verse enabled me to let Christ's peace rule my heart and mind and gave me the courage to endure such a terrifying time.

Learn the Word to live by it. Be kind to yourself if you're like me and don't have the gift of memorization. The point is not how many verses we can quote. God desires that we implant the Word in our minds and hearts so we can apply it to how we live. God isn't pleased with great memories; His greatest pleasure comes when we allow the transforming power of His Word to change us into His likeness.

Scripture Reading: Psalm 119:89, 152; Matthew 5:17-18

Practicing the Spiritual Life

What does God say about the trustworthiness of His Word and its past, present, and future impact on our world?

_____

_____

_____

Learning the Word has an everlasting impact on our lives. Pray about and search for a verse or passage that especially speaks to your needs. Start learning and studying it this week. Note why you chose that particular Scripture.

_____

_____

_____

Prayer

Jesus, I'm so grateful that I've been born again, not of perishable seed, but of imperishable seed, through Your living and enduring Word. For I'm like grass, and all my glory is like the flowers of the field; the grass withers and the flowers fall, but, Lord, Your Word stands forever. Heaven and earth will pass away, but Your words will never pass away. "Your statutes are forever right; give me understanding that I may live." "All your words are true; all your righteous laws are eternal." "Your statutes stand firm; holiness adorns your house for endless days, O Lord." (1 Peter 1:23-24 [see also Isa. 40:8]; Matt. 24:35 paraphrased; Ps. 119:144, 160; 93:5 not paraphrased)

Prayers, Praises, and Personal Notes

_____

_____

_____

Scripture Reading: John 1:1-5, 14-18; 20:30-31

Practicing the Spiritual Life

What does this passage reveal about Christ as the Word? Why was the gospel of John written?

_____

_____

_____

Writing the Word helps implant it in our hearts and minds. Write the verse or passage that you've chosen to learn.

_____

_____

_____

Prayer

O Lord, put Your law in my mind and write it on my heart. For Your Word is living and active. Sharper than any double-edged sword, it penetrates even to dividing soul and spirit, joints and marrow; it judges my thoughts and the attitudes of my heart. Nothing in all creation is hidden from Your sight. Everything is uncovered and laid bare before Your eyes to whom I must give account. I will obey Your precepts and Your statutes, for all my ways are known to You. (Jer. 31:33; Heb. 4:12-13; Ps. 119:168 paraphrased)

Prayers, Praises, and Personal Notes

_____

_____

_____

_____

_____

_____

Scripture Reading: John 5:36-47

Practicing the Spiritual Life
What exhortation did Jesus give regarding Scripture?

_____

_____

_____

How did this passage speak to you about the contrast between studying Scripture and believing in Christ? As you meditate on the passage you're learning, write what you think the Lord desires to teach you.

_____

_____

_____

Prayer
Savior, whatever gain I've had, I will count as loss for Your sake. Indeed I will count everything as loss because of the surpassing worth of knowing You, Lord. For Your sake, even if I suffer the loss of all things, I will count them as refuse, in order that I may gain You and be found in You. O that I may know You, Jesus, and the power of Your resurrection and the fellowship of Your sufferings, being made conformable to Your death; if by any means I might attain unto the resurrection from the dead. For if I am united with You in Your death, I will certainly be united with You in Your resurrection. (Phil. 3:7-9a, 10-11 KJV and RSV; Rom. 6:5 paraphrased)

Prayers, Praises, and Personal Notes

_____

_____

_____

_____

_____

Scripture Reading: 2 Timothy 2:15; 3:14-17

Practicing the Spiritual Life
What did Paul say to Timothy about the Word of God?

_____

_____

_____

Study the Scripture you're learning in different versions of the Bible. Look up key words in a dictionary and/or in a Bible dictionary and commentaries if you have them. Write an amplified version of the verse or passage.

_____

_____

_____

Prayer
May I always keep Your Word with me, to read and study it all the days of my life so that I may learn to revere You, my Lord and my God, and follow carefully all the words of Your law and Your decrees and not consider myself better than other Christians or turn from Your Scripture to the right or to the left. "My heart is set on keeping your decrees to the very end." "I will never forget your precepts, for by them you have preserved my life." (Deut. 17:19-20a paraphrased; Ps. 119:112, 93 not paraphrased)

Prayers, Praises, and Personal Notes

_____

_____

_____

_____

_____

Scripture Reading: Deuteronomy 11:18-21

Practicing the Spiritual Life
What does the Lord ask us to do with Scripture?

_____

_____

_____

We learn God's Word to help us fix it in our minds and hearts and to share it with others. Name those you'd like to share God's Word with. Pray for the Holy Spirit to create a desire in their hearts to know Christ and His Word.

_____

_____

_____

Prayer
"Praise be to you, O Lord; teach me your decrees. With my lips I recount all the laws that come from your mouth. I rejoice in following your statutes as one rejoices in great riches. I meditate on your precepts and consider your ways. I delight in your decrees; I will not neglect your word." By Your grace, I will share Your Word at home, when I walk along the road, when I lie down, and when I get up. (Ps. 119:12-16 not paraphrased; Deut. 6:7b paraphrased)

Prayers, Praises, and Personal Notes

_____

_____

_____

_____

_____

_____

Scripture Reading: Deuteronomy 8:1-6

Practicing the Spiritual Life
Why did God humble the Israelites and allow them to experience physical hunger?

_____

_____

_____

Is there any area of your life where you need to be less concerned about living for material things and more committed to living by the Bread of Life? Write a prayer asking the Lord to feed you with His Word.

_____

_____

_____

Prayer
Jesus, You are the Bread of Life. My forefathers ate the manna in the desert, yet they died. You are the bread that came down from heaven, which I may eat and not die. You are the living bread that came down from heaven. I will eat of this bread and will live forever. This bread is Your flesh, which You gave for my life and the life of the world. Jesus, You are the Bread of my life. I come to You, and I will never go hungry. I believe in You, and I will never be thirsty. When Your words come, I will eat them; they are my joy and my heart's delight, for I bear Your name, O Lord God Almighty. (John 6:48-51, 35; Jer. 15:16 paraphrased)

Prayers, Praises, and Personal Notes

_____

_____

_____

Scripture Reading: Matthew 7:24-27

Practicing the Spiritual Life

What is the difference between the person who lives by the Word and the one who doesn't?

_____

_____

_____

In what ways do you need to build your life on the Rock and practice living by Scripture?

_____

_____

_____

Prayer

Lord Jesus, You alone are my rock and my salvation; You are my fortress; I will never be shaken. I will proclaim Your name. Oh, praise the greatness of my God! You are the Rock; Your works are perfect, and all Your ways are just. You are a faithful God who does no wrong; You are upright and just. There is no one holy like You, Lord; there is no one besides You; there is no Rock like my God. The Lord lives! Praise be to my Rock. Be exalted, O God, the Rock, my Savior. (Ps. 62:2; Deut. 32:3-4; 1 Sam. 2:2; 2 Sam. 22:47 paraphrased)

Prayers, Praises, and Personal Notes

_____

_____

_____

_____

WEEK NINE

Pursue Holiness

*"Since we have these promises,
dear friends, let us purify ourselves from
everything that contaminates body and spirit,
perfecting holiness out of reverence for God."*

2 CORINTHIANS 7:1

$\mathcal{B}$utterflies dance in the air as gracefully as ballerinas. They glide and pirouette and soar to their own melodies. Their beauty is entrancing. When I was young, I chased butterflies until I caught the gloriously colored orange-and-black creatures. Once when I captured one, I felt terrible; when I brushed the iridescent wings, the colors turned to dust. Then I realized that butterflies are fragile and delicate. They quickly die when they're mishandled.

Pursuing holiness reminds me of trying to catch an elusive butterfly. We may capture godliness for a moment, but then it seems to die in our hands. No matter how much we may desire to lead God-honoring lives, we can never seem to capture those qualities without the glorious colors of godliness turning to dusty gray. Even the slightest brush with sin tarnishes the beauty of holiness. Ungodly thoughts. A blatant self-protective lie. A few unkind words. A rude, inconsiderate reaction.

We may rationalize that those sins are minor compared to people's immoral lifestyles. Yet many Christians have adopted those same lifestyles as their own. The twenty-four-hour holocaust of crimes and violence on television, in the movies, and newspapers has desensitized us to the depth of our decay.

A Facade of Faith

Genuine Christians find it more and more difficult to remain faithful when so many are turning away from God or are wearing a facade of faith. We may also struggle with our own falseness and know the sorrow of friends or family members who have turned away from a genuine commitment to Christ.

We have seen in the news or may have been in churches or ministries where leaders made disgraceful choices, leading many astray. Those leaders may use unethical business practices to support their "ministry." They appeal to their audiences using false biblical claims or spiritual manipulation. They seek donations by using fear and guilt tactics, by offering the good life and power through positive living and thinking, and/or making false promises of health and prosperity. They appeal to the needs and hurts of vulnerable people so they can build a mega-ministry, live luxuriously, and satisfy their insatiable lust for more.

Outwardly some people leading and serving in ministries seem devoted. They may be persuasive speakers who grip their hearers' emotions and turn people to tears with their sermons or testimonies. They may preach against the very things they're doing in secret. Their sole purpose in ministry, whether they admit it or not, may be to gain fame and wealth. False Christians include famous authors, evangelists, missionaries, musicians, or preachers and, yes—everyday Christians such as you and me.

Some professing Christians appear to lead godly lives, but, in truth, are leading dark, secret lives. Among them are secret alcoholics, drug addicts, those having affairs, and those who abuse or neglect their own families.

Mixed among those same people are genuine Christians who love and serve their Lord in pure-hearted, godly ways. They are famous Christians, and they are the quietly unknown. They're committed, humble servants of spiritual integrity. They're ethical in their personal and business practices. They're loyal, reliable, and steadfast of faith. The fruit of the Spirit is beautifully evident in the way they love and care for others.

The Empty Life of Unhappy Christians

Unfortunately, superficial Christianity seems popular among many today. Some are convinced that all they need to do is simply believe in Christ and the Bible. They think believing is enough; little else is required. They may outwardly appear to be happy and fulfilled; yet they are leading unhappy, empty lives.

They range from believers who wear a facade of faith, to out-of-fellowship Christians and unbelieving wolves who prey on God's sheep. Superficial Christians or unbelievers may be self-deceived or totally aware of their spiritual condition. They may be in denial and unrealistic about choices destructive to themselves and others. Or they may actually profess that they are living for the Lord while leading ungodly lives. Still others don't dare admit their sins to themselves because they fear they'll lose their salvation.

Some professing believers make wrong seem right. They may claim that their illegal business dealings or the affair they're having with another person is blessed by God. They don't face the pain they're causing by their damaging words and choices. They don't take responsibility for their own actions or their contribution to the problem. Everyone else is wrong.

They may see themselves as victims but may well be the victimizer. They complain bitterly about how they're being treated. Yet they may be hard, unkind, and unfair in their dealings with others.

They may have an addiction or problem unrelated to any bitterness toward people in the church, but they don't feel they can or are unwilling to overcome it. Their guilt and shame may keep them away from God. Or they may deny that they have a sin problem. Or if they do admit their sin, they deny its seriousness. Thoughts of God only remind them of what they're unable to face about themselves.

Unhappy Christians blame others and God for their problems. They believe they have been wounded or wronged, and they may well have been. But they rationalize that they have a right to do wrong or to stop worshiping with other believers, because they feel that God or other Christians have hurt them.

Christians out of fellowship break off relationships with other believers. They're no longer accountable to the Lord and blame Him for everything that has gone wrong in their lives and for not answering their heartfelt prayers. They become extremely bitter toward or critical of other Christians, claiming they're too legalistic or rigid, which may be true. Those who have left their commitment to Christ may say that their lack of faith is due to the hypocritical or offensive behavior of others.

None of us would remain faithful if we used other Christians as a measure for why we should or shouldn't be committed to Christ. Our churches would be empty if we allowed every offense against us to keep us away from fellowshiping with other believers, no matter how truly unfair and hurtful the offense may be.

Even so, we cannot minimize the fact that many Christians have been deeply hurt by the unkind, insensitive, and even cruel actions and remarks of other believers. Due to the condemnatory, judgmental, or rigid attitude of a pastor or the people, many have left churches deeply wounded and don't recover or return to any church again.

Unfortunately, those same Christians often become bitter, hard, and hostile toward the church and genuine faith, because they're unable to forgive.

If they would forgive and release their pain to the Lord, He is more than able to heal them with His tender love. If they would allow God to heal their hurts and sorrows, they could minister to others who have been similarly wounded.

The Secret Life of Genuine Christians

Before we look at the attributes of godly Christians, we need to understand the meaning of holiness. Jerry Bridges wrote, "The best practical definition that I have heard is simply 'without sin.'"[1]

Waging war is the best description of the holy Christian life. We're in a war against ourselves and our own ungodly nature. We're in a war against our constant craving for the good, rich life—for food, money, possessions, and even relationships with people. We're in a war with attitudes and reactions that destroy our commitment to Christ in tough times. We're in a war that requires constant on-duty vigilance to maintain and practice the spiritual disciplines. We're in a war for godliness and against sin—a war that will last until we meet Christ.

Does the holy life seem impossible? Even though we won't fully attain godliness during our lifetime, we can pursue holiness. What then are the secrets of genuine Spirit-controlled Christians? Above all else, they desire to lead holy lives. "God does not require a perfect, sinless life to have fellowship with Him, but He does require that we be serious about holiness, that we grieve over sin in our lives instead of justifying it, and that we earnestly pursue holiness as a way of life."[2]

Genuine Christians recognize that holiness is necessary for effective service to God. Holiness and usefulness are linked together. Unfortunately, God seems to accomplish a great deal even through the ungodly, but it is not a testimony to the person but to God who accomplishes His purposes even through stones if He must (Luke 19:40).

Genuine Christians realize that "to experience practical, everyday holiness, we must accept the fact that God in His infinite wisdom has seen fit to allow this daily battle with indwelling sin. But God does not leave us to do battle alone. Just as He delivered us from the overall reign of sin, so He has made ample provision for us to win the daily skirmishes against sin."[3] This means that we have not only been delivered from sin's hold on us, but we have been made alive to God and *are united with Christ in all His power.* It is certainly true we cannot live a holy life in our own strength. Christianity is not a do-it-yourself thing."[4]

How then do we pursue holiness? First, we need to develop the discipline of choices. We need to face our sins realistically, confess our wrongs, ask forgiveness, and change our attitudes, actions, or speech.

This can be particularly discouraging for those of us who have lost the battle repeatedly to certain sins, who have discovered new ones entangling our minds and actions faster than sprouting weeds. Or we may add destructive attitudes or habits in place of old ones we conquered. Or old ones may take over after we thought we had finally gained control over them. Sometimes we wonder if we'll ever gain the victory we desire.

"A second implication of being alive to God is that *He has given us His Holy Spirit to live within us.*" [5] The disciplines of being Spirit-controlled, pursuing holiness, and faithfully feeding on the Word of God are inseparable links.

Expressing our dependence on the Holy Spirit to lead a holy life can be done in several ways. The first is to consistently study Scripture and meditate on it. "There really is no other way to know God than through the revelation of his Word by the illumination of the Holy Spirit. If Scripture is not the centerpiece of your quiet time, then it will not impart the supernatural life that every word of God contains." [6]

The second is to pursue the disciplined, Spirit-controlled life and to yield to the Holy Spirit's guidance and direction. "The mind controlled by the Spirit views all of life from God's perspective. It is constantly nourished by the Word of God and is focused on the priority of spiritual principles above the philosophy and mind-set of the world. It filters all of our thoughts, emotions, and contemplations through the pure grid of the Scriptures. Our minds are yielded to the Spirit's influence and direction." [7]

The third is to pursue holiness no matter how often we fail and to remain accountable to committed Christians. Their prayers, convicting counsel, and spiritual wisdom can help us maintain godliness.

Finally, we're entirely dependent on the Spirit of God to enable us to overcome our sins and grow in holiness even when we think we can't possibly do so. "We are both personally responsible and totally dependent in our practice of godliness. . . . The principle of simultaneous personal responsibility and total dependence upon God for fulfillment is one of the most important principles in the practice of godliness." [8]

Bridges also notes that when we sin, we're often upset by our embarrassment, failure, and the lowering of our self-esteem rather than being grieved that we have dishonored God. Therefore, "our desire for holiness, our motivation to pursue it, must be a God-centered desire and motivation" rather than being concerned about our self-image.[9]

Realistically, it sometimes seems easier to give up. How can we possibly maintain holiness when we're so tired of fighting our own inner compulsions, when we're embarrassed by our lack of spiritual desire or commitment to lead holy lives? How can we be godly when we wander in the desert of despair, when we lose heart because the trials are so great and our losses so senseless?

During those times we need to ask God to hang on to us, because we can't hold on ourselves. Our Lord offers us this encouragement, "Let us not become weary in doing good, for at the proper time we will reap a harvest if we do not give up" (Gal. 6:9).

Here's another promise to take as your own; keep it close to your heart and in your thoughts: "'You are my servant'; I have chosen you and have not rejected you. So do not fear, for I am with you; do not be dismayed, for I am your God. I will strengthen you and help you; I will uphold you with my righteous right hand" (Isa. 41:9b-10).

How then can we give up seeking godliness when the Comforter has promised to minister to our deepest hurts and to use our sorrow to comfort others in their own grief (2 Cor. 1:3-4)? How can we give up when Jesus gave His life for us that we might live to glorify Him and have everlasting life? How can we give up when the Holy Spirit is always available to empower us to keep on pursuing holiness?

Scripture Reading: Leviticus 11:44a; 2 Corinthians 7:1

Practicing the Spiritual Life

What is our call to lead a holy life based on? How do we obtain holiness?

Write a prayer asking the Lord to give you the desire to seek a more holy life.

Prayer

I know that my body is Your temple—Your very sanctuary—O Holy Spirit, who lives within me, whom I have received as a gift from You, Father God. I am not my own; You bought me at a price. Therefore, help me to honor You in my body, mind, and speech. By Your ever-merciful grace, I will consecrate myself and be holy because You are the Lord my God. I will keep Your decrees and follow them, for You are the One, the only One, who makes me holy. (1 Cor. 6:19-20 AMP; Lev. 20:7-8 paraphrased)

Prayers, Praises, and Personal Notes

Scripture Reading: Titus 2:11-14

Practicing the Spiritual Life

The above passage speaks about the discipline of choices. What does it say we're to do regarding godliness?

_____

_____

_____

Often we say we want to overcome certain sins, but we honestly don't have the desire or commitment. Or maybe we've failed so many times we've given up. In what area of your life do you need the renewed desire, self-control, and commitment to overcome sin?

_____

_____

_____

Prayer

May godly sorrow bring me to repentance that leads to deliverance and leaves no regrets, for worldly sorrow brings death. If I conceal my sins, I will not prosper, but I will confess and renounce them and find Your mercy. I will wash my hands, for I am a sinner, and purify my heart, for I am double-minded. I belong to You, Jesus, so I will crucify my sinful nature with its passions and desires. In accordance with Your great love, forgive my sins. (2 Cor. 7:10; James 4:8b; Gal. 5:24; Num. 14:19a paraphrased)

Prayers, Praises, and Personal Notes

_____

_____

_____

_____

Scripture Reading: John 16:5-15; Galatians 5:16-18

Practicing the Spiritual Life

In what ways does the Holy Spirit work in our lives and in the world? How does the Galatians passage contrast living by the Spirit to living by the sinful nature?

_____

_____

_____

The Spirit-controlled discipline means that we yield to the Holy Spirit's guidance. Name specific areas of your life in which you need the Spirit's direction, and note how He leads you.

_____

_____

_____

Prayer

O Holy God, I have not received the spirit of the world but the Spirit who is from You that I may understand what You have freely given me. Now may Your Spirit rest on me—Your Spirit of wisdom and of understanding, Your Spirit of counsel and of power, Your Spirit of knowledge and of the fear of You, Lord. (1 Cor. 2:12; Isa. 11:2 paraphrased)

Prayers, Praises, and Personal Notes

_____

_____

_____

_____

_____

_____

Scripture Reading: Ephesians 4:17–5:18

Practicing the Spiritual Life

We are called to pursue holiness and put off sin. What are some of the sins we're to take off?

_____

_____

_____

The Holy Spirit empowers us to replace old behaviors and thoughts with godly ones. Ask the Holy Spirit to reveal to you any sin that may be defeating you. Make a specific time commitment, such as a week or a month. Set a date when you will reevaluate how you're doing and what you may or may not need to continue doing to overcome that sin.

_____

_____

_____

Prayer

O Lord, deliver me from all that corrupts my mind, robs me of the truth, and causes me to think that godliness is a means to financial gain. For godliness with contentment is great gain. I brought nothing into the world, and I can take nothing out of it. As Your servant, I will flee from all this and pursue righteousness, godliness, faith, love, endurance, and gentleness. I will fight the good fight of faith. (1 Tim. 6:5b-7, 11-12a paraphrased)

Prayers, Praises, and Personal Notes

_____   _____

_____   _____

_____

_____

Scripture Reading: Ephesians 4:32–5:2, 15-21; 2 Peter 1:3-4

Practicing the Spiritual Life

List some of the ways we are to lead a holy life. What has the Lord given us so that we may be godly, according to 2 Peter?

_____

_____

_____

Choose several of the godly attitudes and actions that you would like to begin incorporating into your life. Set a specific goal date, and check your progress at that time.

_____

_____

_____

Prayer

Jesus, I will make every effort to add to my faith goodness; and to goodness, knowledge; and to knowledge, self-control; and to self-control, perseverance; and to perseverance, godliness; and to godliness, brotherly kindness; and to brotherly kindness, love. For if I possess these qualities in increasing measure, they will keep me from being ineffective in my knowledge of You, Lord. But if I do not make every effort to have these qualities, I am nearsighted and blind and have forgotten that I have been cleansed from my past sins. Therefore, I will be all the more eager to make my calling and election sure. For if I do these things, I will never fall, and I will receive a rich welcome into Your eternal kingdom. (2 Peter 1:5-11 paraphrased)

Prayers, Praises, and Personal Notes

_____

_____

_____

Scripture Reading: Philippians 1:6; 2:13; 2 Timothy 1:11-14

Practicing the Spiritual Life

What has the Lord promised regarding His work in our lives?

_____

_____

_____

In what areas of your life do you need to be responsible and yet dependent upon the Lord so that He can continue a good work in your life and help you practice the Spirit-controlled discipline?

_____

_____

_____

Prayer

Spirit of God, may I always keep in mind and constantly pray that You may count me worthy of Your calling and that by Your power You may fulfill every good purpose of Yours and every act prompted by faith. I will continue to pray this so that Your name, Lord Jesus, may be glorified in me, and I in You, according to Your grace. For who among the gods is like You, O Lord? Who is like You—majestic in holiness, awesome in glory, working wonders? By Your unfailing love You will lead me, for You have redeemed me. By Your strength You will guide me to Your holy dwelling. (2 Thess. 1:11-12; Ex. 15:11, 13 paraphrased)

Prayers, Praises, and Personal Notes

_____

_____

_____

_____

Scripture Reading: Isaiah 6:1-3; Revelation 4:8-11

Practicing the Spiritual Life

What do the creatures of heaven acknowledge about God and for what do they praise Him?

_____

_____

_____

Write praises to our ever-loving, holy Savior God for who He is.

_____

_____

_____

Prayer

You are great, Lord, and most worthy of praise; You are to be feared above all gods. For all the gods of the nations are idols, but You made the heavens. Splendor and majesty are before You; strength and joy are in your dwelling place. I ascribe to You, O holy Savior, glory and strength. I ascribe to You the glory due Your name. I bring an offering of praise and come before You; I worship You, Lord, in the splendor of Your holiness. (1 Chron. 16:25-29 paraphrased)

Prayers, Praises, and Personal Notes

_____

_____

_____

_____

_____

_____

Place Yourself in God's Presence

*"Draw near to God and he will
draw near to you."*

JAMES 4:8A RSV

*T*oday's needs are yesterday's unheard-of luxuries. The explosion of inventions to make our lives easier has, instead, made our lives more complicated and harder to manage. The demands of keeping up with and maintaining the ever-increasing luxury items that fill our homes or dreams consume our time.

It's not just the demands of luxury items and things, but people consume our energy. The people we work with and/or our families and friends have needs. Our own desires often conflict with our sense of duty to meet their needs.

And it's not just the demands of things and people, but the lure of new activities, of new opportunities. There's so much to choose from and participate in, so many classes offering every possible subject from the arts to computers to zoology and seminars promoting new gimmicks to get rich, lose weight, or lead healthy lives. Dozens of recreational or sports activities are available for us to watch or play. A barrage of books, magazines, newspapers, and television programs entice us to give our devoted attention. Our relationship with God and church activities also beckon us.

Life is no longer simple. We're overloaded with numerous opportunities and ordinary demands. We may become so overwhelmed by all there is to do that we feel exhausted and deprived of time for ourselves. Yet how often do we stop and count the number of hours we spend maintaining what we own, meeting people's needs, sitting in front of the television, or doing other extra activities. We may want to do it all and don't understand why we can't.

Finally, it's not just the demands of things, people, and activities but the ever-increasing crime and frightening violence that commands our attention and causes us to feel anxious and constantly vigilant. Safe places to live no longer exist. We worry about our loved ones, our children, grandchildren, and our own lives. Living is far more complicated than it ever has been in the history of our world.

As a result, "our lives are fragmented. There are so many things to do, so many events to worry about, so many people to think of, so many experiences to work through, so many tasks to fulfill, so many demands to respond to, and so many needs to pay attention to. Often it seems that just keeping things together asks for enormous energy. . . . This fragmentation is probably one of the most painful experiences of modern men and women."[1]

Due to our fragmented lives and the fears that plague us, many of us desire a quieter, simpler existence. We long for peaceful, less complicated lives, but we can't seem to escape the bombardment of demands, the trials, broken people, or our own brokenness and compulsions.

Some of us have become sick of things and sick of our own desire for them. But we don't know how to break the bondage of our lust for luxuries that only leave us empty and dissatisfied after we've worked so hard to obtain them. We seek comfort in what we buy, in what we create, in what we crave rather than in the Creator. We try to satisfy our anxieties and stress with human comforts rather than seeking our Holy Comforter's ever-present help.

Seeking God in the Center of a Cyclone

How can we possibly develop the discipline of continuously placing ourselves in God's presence when this technological age jets by us at a supersonic speed? How can we continually speak with our Lord and dearest Friend throughout every waking moment and seek His guidance regarding what He would have us do at this present moment when so many demands tug at us?

How can we practice the presence of God as Brother Lawrence did in the 1600s, living in the quiet, sheltered community of a monastery when our world is so chaotic and radically different? Those questions are not easy ones to answer. Yet they're important to consider if we're going to strengthen our walk with God and find spiritual support in tough times.

First, let us take a brief look into the life and writings of the man who left us the discipline of practicing the presence of God. Brother Lawrence was a humble, simple brother who lived in a Carmelite monastery. In the mid-1600s a collection of interviews, letters, and miscellaneous writings of Brother Lawrence were published as *The Practice of the Presence of God*. The book has remained in print ever since then, and it has continued to challenge Christians to develop the discipline of practicing God's presence.

Speaking constantly with our Lord in the center of our cyclone lives is an even greater challenge today than it has ever been, but it is also needed more than ever. If we're going to remain spiritually strong, if we're going to remain committed to Christ, we need to develop this habit. What Brother Lawrence has to say seems so simple but is so difficult, as those of us know who have attempted to practice this discipline.

Placing Ourselves in God's Presence

The idea of "practicing the presence of God" puzzled me for a long time, since God is always present with us whether we realize it or not. He may seem distant and even uncaring, though in reality He is always close to us. I finally came to realize that we need to place ourselves in His presence and continually practice seeking Him because our own pain, our own questions, our own unanswered prayers cause us to feel distant from Him.

Jesus is our tender, compassionate Shepherd who cares about us and understands the distance we may feel from Him. He desires that we experience His comforting presence. Yet when we're grieving, it's more difficult to open ourselves to Him, because we're so hurt by the pain He's allowed us to experience.

Brother Lawrence has many simple yet profound insights to teach us about the spiritual disciplines, how to practice God's presence and develop a deep personal friendship with Him. I've also shared some of my own struggles from the past few years in seeking the Lord's presence (in italics):

Brother Lawrence said, "The holiest, most common, most necessary practice in the spiritual life is the presence of God, that is, to take delight in and become accustomed to His divine company, speaking humbly and talking lovingly with Him at all times, at every moment, without rule or system, and especially in times of temptation, suffering, spiritual aridity, disgust and even of unfaithfulness and sin"[2]

How often my thoughts about God and my prayers turn into agitated internal complaints or angry diatribes. How often I get out the "history book" of past hurts or difficult experiences and relive them in my mind. How can I be at peace and seek God's presence if I don't let go of past hurts, past painful relationships, and past wrongs? In constantly trying to think of the Lord and speaking to Him, I've learned more about my own thought life, how it controls me and how off-center it can sometimes be.

Brother Lawrence worked for fifteen years in the kitchen, "for which he had a naturally strong aversion." At the end of his life he worked in the shoe repair shop. He said that he was "very happy there but that he was ready to leave this position as he had previous ones, glad to do any task, however small, for the love of God. . . . That he found the best way of reaching God was by doing ordinary tasks, which he was obliged to perform under obedience, entirely for the love of God and not for the human attitude toward them."[3]

What spoke to me most about this was how willingly Brother Lawrence worked at jobs he intensely disliked and would never have chosen to do. But he learned to do any menial task for the love of God. I find my own life taken up with work and problems I would never have chosen. I not only dislike them but feel angry at even having to deal with them. Life's troubles disrupt my plans and cast me into situations or duties I'd never choose myself. I'd rather do what I desire than the hard tasks. May God give me the grace to do all my duties and tasks as a loving gift to others and for His glory. May His gracious love shine through all that I do.

"That when the occasion arose to practice some virtue he always said to God: 'My God, I cannot do this unless You enable me to do so,' and he was immediately given the strength needed, and even more. That when he had stumbled, he simply acknowledged his fault and said to God: 'I shall never do otherwise if You leave me to myself; it is up to You to keep me from falling and to correct what is wrong.' With this he put the pain of this fault from his mind."[4]

I, too, fall constantly, forgetting God easily as I go about my daily life, falling often into wrongful thoughts. Yet I'm so hard on myself. Brother Lawrence's simple confession reminds me of how the Lord desires that I come to Him with the same childlike trust and confidence and then put the fault from my mind. I clutch guilt, embarrassment, and shame while Brother Lawrence confessed his sins, let them go, and simply returned to his conversations with His Lord.

"We must continually work hard so that each of our actions is a way of carrying on little conversations with God, not in any carefully prepared way but as it comes from the purity and simplicity of the heart. . . . I keep myself in His presence by simple attentiveness and a loving gaze upon God, which I can call the actual presence of God or to put it more clearly, an habitual, silent and secret conversation of the soul with God."[5]

The secret is carrying on conversations with the Lord while I'm working and while doing every menial task. I realize that this means talking to the Lord at all times and in all places, not just during my devotions or in prayer or at church. Every hour can become a time of constant communion, adoration, and intercession for others.

"God is a spirit, therefore, He must be worshiped in spirit and in truth; that is to say, by a humble and genuine act of adoration from the very depths of our soul. Only God can see this adoration, which if repeated often will eventually become natural for us as if God were one with our soul and our soul one with God: practice will make us understand this."[6]

I've been trying to seek His company. I sing hymns and songs in the car, but I've felt that much of what I do is intellectual and not heartfelt. It's "surface" rather than a deep and genuine conversation with God. That is a lie of Satan, I've decided. I may need to begin with the mind and the intellect in practicing God's presence, in singing songs and hymns to Him, in thinking about Him. The Lord will help me with practice to turn my thoughts into heartfelt devotion.

When I sing the same song over and over or say the same verse or prayer, I fear it is nothing more than vain repetition, a mere babbling of words. May the Lord help me to find balance. Singing the same song to the Lord or repeating the same verse does deliver me from anger, bitterness, depression, fear, spiteful thoughts, and ungodly imaginations. I pray that what I say to the Lord and my heartfelt devotion will become one.

"We must carry out all of our actions with care and with wisdom, without . . . a distraught mind; it is necessary to work peacefully, tranquilly, and lovingly with God, begging Him to accept our work, and by this continual mindfulness of God we shall crush the head of the devil and cause his weapons to fall from his hands."[7]

Two thoughts came to mind regarding practicing God's presence. What would God have me do now, today, this week? Am I making the best use of His time? So often I think of time as my own. I'm always struggling to finish what I should do, the ordinary duties, so that I am free to do what I want to do. Hurry and finish this or that mundane task so I can get to what I enjoy. All of this, of course, leaves God out. In practicing His presence, I've become more aware of how I use His time, of what He would have me do instead of what I want to do.

"During our work and other activities, during our spiritual reading and writing, even more so during our formal devotions and spoken prayers we should stop as often as we can, for a moment, to adore God from the bottom of our hearts, to savor Him. . . . These interior retreats to God gradually free us by destroying that self-love which can exist only among our fellow human beings."[8]

How I pray that I may increase more and more in adoring God. How quickly my prayers turn to self and family concerns.

"All these acts of adoration should be made by faith, knowing that God is truly in our hearts, that we must adore, love and serve Him in spirit and in truth, that He sees everything that happens and will happen to us and to all His creatures, that He is independent of everything and all creatures depend on Him. . . ."[9]

Offering constant adoration doesn't change the reality that my trials exist. Praise and thanksgiving lift me out of my concerns and my concentration on my own needs and into His joyous presence.

Scripture Reading: Psalm 139

Practicing the Spiritual Life

What does this psalm say about God being present in our lives?

_____

_____

_____

Write about a time when you felt that God's presence was especially with you.

_____

_____

_____

Prayer

Are You only a God nearby and not a God far away? Can I hide in secret places so that You cannot see me? No, I cannot hide from You, for You fill heaven and earth. This day I acknowledge and take to heart that You, Lord, are in heaven above and on the earth below. There is no other God. My ways are in full view of You, Lord, and You examine all my paths. You see my ways and count my every step. Thank You for watching over me as a shepherd watches over his flock. (Jer. 23:23-24; Deut. 4:39; Prov. 5:21; Job 31:4, 10b paraphrased)

Prayers, Praises, and Personal Notes

_____

_____

_____

_____

_____

Scripture Reading: John 14:16-17; Romans 8:8-17

Practicing the Spiritual Life

What does the Word say about the Holy Spirit's presence in our lives?

Set specific times throughout the day and evening when you will begin pursuing the Lord's presence and seeking the Holy Spirit's guidance.

Prayer

O Holy God, You redeemed me in order that the blessing given to Abraham might come to me through You, so that by faith I might receive the promise of the Spirit. Lord God, I know that I live in You, and You live in me, because You have given me of Your Spirit. I know that I am Your temple and that Your Spirit lives in me. You are always with me; You hold me by my right hand. You guide me with Your counsel. Now help me to speak, not in words taught to me by human wisdom, but in words taught by You, Holy Spirit, so that I may express spiritual truths in spiritual words. (Gal. 3:14; 1 John 4:13; 1 Cor. 3:16; Ps. 73:23-24a; 1 Cor. 2:13 paraphrased)

Prayers, Praises, and Personal Notes

Scripture Reading: Psalm 145:18-20

Practicing the Spiritual Life

What does God promise about being near to us?

_____

_____

_____

Do you feel God is far away from you because of a particular concern or difficulty? If so, write a note asking Him for the assurance of His unfailing presence during this time of need.

_____

_____

_____

Prayer

I call on You, O God, for You will answer me; give ear to me and hear my prayer. Show the wonder of Your great love, You who save by Your right hand those who take refuge in You from their foes. As for me, it is good to be near You, Lord. I have made You my refuge. You are my Shepherd who gathers me as a lamb in Your arms, carries me close to Your heart, and gently leads me. Your eyes are on me because I fear You; my hope is in Your unfailing love. Keep me as the apple of Your eye; hide me in the shadow of Your wings. (Ps. 17:6-7; 73:28a; Isa. 40:11; Ps. 33:18; 17:8 paraphrased)

Prayers, Praises, and Personal Notes

_____

_____

_____

_____

Scripture Reading: Hebrews 10:22-23

Practicing the Spiritual Life
How are we to draw near to God?

_____

_____

_____

Is anything in your life preventing you from having a sincere heart for God and full assurance of faith?

_____

_____

_____

Prayer
Lord, it is my desire to have a conscience that testifies that I have conducted myself in the world, and especially in my relations with others, in the holiness and sincerity that are from You. May I not live according to worldly wisdom but according to Your grace. For the wisdom that comes from heaven is first of all pure, then peace loving, considerate, submissive, full of mercy and good fruit, impartial, and sincere. Now help me to be watchful, to stand firm in my faith, to be courageous and strong. May all that I do be done in love. (2 Cor. 1:12; James 3:17; 1 Cor. 16:13-14 RSV paraphrased)

Prayers, Praises, and Personal Notes

_____

_____

_____

_____

Scripture Reading: Psalm 31:19-24

Practicing the Spiritual Life

When we take refuge in God and seek His presence, what does He promise us?

_____

_____

_____

Are you feeling besieged by problems and cut off from God? If so, present your difficulties to Him.

_____

_____

_____

Prayer

O Lord, You are a shield around me, my Glorious One, who lifts up my head. To You I cry aloud, and You answer me from Your holy hill. I lie down and sleep, and I wake again because You sustain me. I wait in hope for You, Lord; You are my help and my shield. From You alone comes deliverance. May Your blessing be on me. In You my heart rejoices, for I trust in Your holy name. May Your unfailing love rest upon me, O Lord, even as I put my hope in You. (Ps. 3:3-5; 33:20; 3:8; 33:21-22 paraphrased)

Prayers, Praises, and Personal Notes

_____

_____

_____

_____

Scripture Reading: Psalm 42:1-8

Practicing the Spiritual Life

How did the psalmist seek God? What experience did he have of God's presence during times when he felt downcast?

_____

_____

_____

Daily pursuing the Lord as you do ordinary tasks will help you establish a close, loving relationship with Him. Then when you experience heartaches, you will feel His comfort more than you ever have before. In what concerns do you need the assurance of His constant, caring presence?

_____

_____

_____

Prayer

Lord, You are my refuge and strength, an ever-present help in trouble. Therefore I will not fear, though the earth give way, and the mountains fall into the heart of the sea, though its waters roar and foam, and the mountains quake with their surging. I will be still and know that You are God. For You are with me, Lord Almighty; You are my fortress, God of Jacob. Surely, You will be with me always to the very end of the age. (Ps. 46:1-3, 10a, 11; Matt. 28:20b paraphrased)

Prayers, Praises, and Personal Notes

_____

_____

_____

Scripture Reading: Psalm 35:28; 95:1-7

Practicing the Spiritual Life

In what ways are we to practice God's presence through praise?

_____

_____

_____

Write praises to the Lord for all that He is doing in your life, and then practice His presence by worshiping Him.

_____

_____

_____

Prayer

I will sing to You all my life, Lord; I will sing praise to You, my God as long as I live. May my meditation be pleasing to You as I rejoice in You. I will constantly tell of all Your wonderful acts. I will glory in Your holy name; my heart seeks You and rejoices. "I thank and praise you, O God of my fathers." I exalt You and worship at Your footstool; You are holy. I worship You, Lord, in the splendor of Your holiness. Praise be to Your name forever and ever, for wisdom and power are Yours. (Ps. 104:33-34; 105:2b-3 paraphrased; Dan. 2:23a not paraphrased; Ps. 99:5; 96:9a; Dan. 2:20 paraphrased)

Prayers, Praises, and Personal Notes

_____

_____

_____

_____

_____

WEEK ELEVEN

Present Yourself for Service

> *"I know your deeds, your love and faith,
> your service and perseverance,
> and that you are now doing
> more than you did at first."*

REVELATION 2:19

We're living in the present moment, though most of the time our thoughts are centered on the past or what must be done in the future. God, however, is more concerned about what we do at this moment than what we do tomorrow. If we keep doing what God wants us to do now, we'll accomplish His desires for a lifetime.

As we've discovered, practicing God's presence is constantly talking with the Lord as if He's our dearest friend. It means praising and worshiping Him as we go about our daily business. Present-moment service is seeking God's guidance, listening for what He desires of us, and responding to His directions at all times.[1]

But we often separate the secular from the sacred. Our regular work is not considered a service to the Lord. Some Christians also believe that pastors, missionaries, and ministry staff are the only ones called to full-time service. If we do volunteer ministry, we often consider it a specific service that we do at a church or a particular place. We have a prescribed definition of Christian ministry, but we don't think of our daily duties as a way of serving God.

We view ordinary tasks as no more than the means to maintain life. Yet it's how we seek God's guidance every moment, how we minister to and love those we live and work with, how we yield to God's desires in the smallest of tasks that really counts. Those same duties may well be the ones God presently desires us to do for Him. When we're seeking and obeying His guidance, every mundane duty, every great or small task, everything we do at any given moment can become sacred acts of service.

"The requirements of a work to be done can be understood as the will of God. If I am supposed to hoe a garden or make a table, then I will be obeying God if I am true to the task I am performing. To do the work carefully and well, with love and respect for the nature of my task and with due attention to its purposes, is to unite myself to God's will in my work."[2]

Serving God in our daily work, however, doesn't negate a call to a specific place of ministry—rather it strengthens that call. But how do we know the ways God wants us to serve Him? What ministry should we be doing?

"The word *will* as in 'God's will' comes from a Greek word that carries feeling and even passion. When we say 'What is God's will?' we are asking, 'What is God's deep, heartfelt desire for our lives and our world? What does this God who loves us want for us above all? What is God committed to accomplishing on our behalf no matter what the cost?'"[3]

Those are questions that only God can answer for each one of us. How, where, and with whom the Lord calls us to daily minister is as individual and unique as we are.

God Calls All to Serve

The following spiritual principles offer us a guide to the ways God calls us to seek His daily guidance and to serve Him and others:

God calls us to present-moment service. This takes constant awareness of whom we're with or what we're doing at the present moment. Whom does God want me to help or speak to now? What hard or easy task can I do for His glory?

Present-moment service doesn't replace a ministry we're already doing. It means that we remain open to surprise opportunities to share the Lord while we're serving. Rather than being totally focused on the service we're doing and what we've determined to accomplish, we listen for the Holy Spirit's guidance about what He would have us do this minute.

We also need to be wary of becoming caught up in the tyranny of the urgent, so that we only meet emergencies and miss other needs that are just as critical. This is where wisdom and spiritual discernment are so vital. It's knowing when to say yes or no to what we're asked to do. It means we may need to continue what we're doing instead of responding to every crisis or opportunity to serve.

God calls us to seek Him daily in order to serve Him daily. Through our devotional time and as we constantly carry on a conversation with the Lord and listen for His still, small voice throughout the day, we'll become more and more tuned to what He desires of us. We'll know how to lovingly serve others as we trust Him to give us the guidance we need.

God calls us to be His servants by daily taking up our cross and following Him. Jesus said, "'Whoever wants to become great among you must be your servant, and whoever wants to be first must be your slave—just as the Son of

Man did not come to be served, but to serve, and to give his life as a ransom for many'" (Matt. 20:26b-28).

"What is the cross? It is, I believe, the thing required of me today. 'Let him take up his cross daily,' Jesus said, 'and follow me.' Some duty lies on my doorstep right now. It may be a simple thing that I have known for a long time I ought to do, but it has been easy to avoid. It is probably the thing that springs to my mind when I pray. . . . It may be that although I have been doing something I ought to do, I have never done it without grudging. The so-called 'cross' which I could not avoid I may, for a change, take up with gladness. Might I not then, for the first time, be on the way to true discipleship?"[4]

God calls us to serve Him by spending less time and money on ourselves so we can give more of both to the church, to missionaries, and to those in need. This means we work to overcome our addiction to spending our time doing what we please, overworking to achieve all that we can, and striving for more possessions. In our you-can-have-it-all materialistic society, it's extremely difficult to overcome the compulsion to do and to acquire more. Maintaining our possessions can become an all-consuming task. If only we could learn "to enjoy things without owning them."[5]

God calls us to serve Him according to His time frame, not our own. Elisabeth Elliot wrote, "I realize that nearly all of my trouble with finding out the will of God came because I wanted it too soon. . . . My acceptance of his timing was a rigorous exercise in trust. . . . I would always ask desperately to be shown God's will, but he never showed it to me until the time came. And when it came, it was as clear as the sunlight."[6]

God's call to serve is a daily process, not a product of our life or ministry. We may encounter disappointments when we serve the Lord, because we had our mind set on how a particular ministry should turn out. We may spend hours planning and preparing for a ministry event, but one or more key persons don't follow through and do what they promised.

It's our expectations of what God should do and how people should perform that disillusion us. That's why many Christians give up, feel burned out, and refuse to serve. If we let go of our expectations and change our focus to whom we can minister to, we'll have the joy of seeing God work small miracles. The Lord is honored and glorified by our loving obedience even though the outcome may be disappointing or far different from what we had expected.

In a similar sense if the person we've devoted many hours ministering to doesn't commit to faith in Christ or turns away from Him, we need to trust that God already knows and understands. When we consider the ministries of Jesus, the disciples and the Apostle Paul, we see that some people didn't believe in Christ or faithfully follow Him at all. We and/or those we serve may fail to be committed to the Savior, but He always remains faithful.

Discovering God's Guidance

God guides us and shows us where and how to serve Him through divine appointments. The Lord leads us by the Holy Spirit's guidance and by directing us to different Bible passages, Christian books, people, or through circumstances and trials. Each new day brings unexpected opportunities to see our Lord at work. During our devotions or in a simple conversation, God will speak to us about how we can serve Him and others at that moment. Or we may unexpectedly be able to share what God is doing in our lives with another person. God has many divine appointments for us; we need only to keep them.

God has multiplied purposes for our lives. He desires that we serve Him in numerous different ways. Our service for the Lord, what He daily teaches us, how He strengthens our faith, the ways we grow spiritually, and the trials we experience are not just for our benefit alone but to serve others. And what the Lord does in the lives of others is for our benefit as well.

God has many purposes for each ministry we do, for each trial we go through, for each way He ministers to us in our own needs. If we're aware, open, and sensitive to the leading of the Holy Spirit, He'll show us the many surprising ways He can use one experience.

Herb, a friend of ours, has AIDS. The Lord has transformed him, redeemed his life, and used him in numerous ways by giving him a ministry to others with AIDS and to their families. Because Herb has been open and willingly shared God's grace in his life, many people have committed their lives to Christ, renewed their faith, been ministered to while they were dying, and gained the courage they needed to face such a dreaded disease.

Leona, my dearest friend, and I have had parallel experiences both in ministry and in our personal lives. It seems as if one of us goes through certain experiences or trials before the other one does. We gain from what the

Lord is teaching each other. When I see God's faithfulness to Leona as she goes through a trial, and then I later go through a similar one, I know that God has seen her through such a difficult time, and He'll see me through my own. Out of what we've been through, we can share the Lord's faithfulness to us with others to encourage them and give them hope for their own tough times.

God asks us to seek His guidance and then serve Him according to His plans, not our own. "It is not reasonable to ask for guidance in one matter if we are aware that in another matter we have rejected the guidance already given. Let us first go back, if possible, to where we turned away. If this is no longer possible, let us confess our sin."[7]

The hardest place of service, the one that tests our obedience the most, is doing what we don't want to do even though the Lord has made it plain to us that we should. And if we do that service with a bitter, begrudging attitude, we'll do harm to the name of Christ and hurt others in the process. This is when we need to will to do God's will with open hands and a loving heart.

God may use other people to affirm His place of service for us. In seeking guidance, "we ought to look first of all to those with whom we have some special relationship. . . . God works always with perfect wisdom, always with perfect love, and nearly always in conjunction with human means."[8]

Sadly, many have "served the Lord" in volunteer church activities or full-time ministries when they were totally unsuited for the job. They dogmatically held onto what they thought was the call of God for their life when it was obvious to those who knew them that they didn't belong where they were serving.

While others may be well suited for a ministry position, they don't believe they are. We don't see ourselves as others see us; we're often blind to our strengths and weaknesses and to our gifts or lack of abilities. We need the counsel and wisdom of others in determining what God would have us do to serve Him, whether it be volunteer or full time. We may feel the strong leading of the Lord, but our feelings are not always an accurate gauge. We also cannot consider how much we enjoy doing something as a measure of where we should serve. We may enjoy doing certain ministries, but we still aren't called to do them or may be unsuited for the task.

On the other hand, we may not enjoy doing some services, but that's exactly where we belong. God has called me numerous times to serve Him in ways that

I'd never have chosen. The confirmation of God and others who believed I had a gift in certain areas has led me to ministries I couldn't imagine doing. Finally, we may be well suited for a ministry, but God hasn't called us to that place. God has soundly shut the door for me to serve in ministries that I had a great desire to do and that others believed I should be doing too. Now I can look back over the years and see that God's choices were the wisest ones.

A Personal Journey in Accepting God's Plans

Many of us wish God would write us a personal letter or fly a banner across the sky with clear directions. Finding how and where God would have us serve isn't easy. As we've already discovered, His place of service for us may not be the place we would choose.

Several years ago, I was working for a ministry as a book editor and thought I would be serving there for my remaining working years. Then the ministry unexpectedly announced they were moving out of state. My heart's desire was to move with the ministry, but God was making it very clear that it wasn't His choice for my life.

During a seven-day period God affirmed His will for me about our decision not to move. While on a brief vacation and a few days following it, the Lord ministered to me in special ways, showing me that He would guide me to new places of service. A couple of those days, I spent several hours having a quiet retreat reading the Word. Verse after verse was on the shepherd theme and how God loves, comforts, and guides us. The Lord spoke to me in incredible ways. By divine coincidence the weekly hymn in my devotional book was the one with the words I needed: "Savior, like a shepherd lead us, Much we need thy tender care; In thy pleasant pastures feed us, For our use thy folds prepare. . . . We are thine, do thou befriend us, be the guardian of our way. . . . Thou hast loved us, love us still."

Saturday Ron and I looked for a church to attend Sunday and had decided on one near where we were staying. That evening we learned about another church, one we would never have known about because it was out of the way, but we decided to attend it.

Sunday I was astounded when the usher handed me the worship service bulletin. The theme for the morning service was "The Lord is my Shepherd." The hymns were "All the Way My Savior Leads Me," "He Leadeth Me," and "Savior, Like a Shepherd Lead Us." The title of the message was "It's Okay to Be a Sheep When You Have a Good Shepherd."

One of the verses used during worship was "In your unfailing love you will lead the people you have redeemed" (Ex. 15:13). I cried openly in that service; I was so moved by the Lord's outpouring of love to me and His promise that he would care for and guide me.

The following Monday morning before work, my readings and several different verses were about God's love. The hymn for the week was "Love Divine, all loves excelling . . . Breathe, O breathe thy loving Spirit into every troubled breast."

Tuesday morning I arose to have devotions, wondering how the Lord would send me off to work. I'd awakened at 3:30 A.M. due to a sleep disorder and a stress reaction to other difficult trials. The Lord reminded me to rejoice in those sufferings, because they produce perseverance, character, and hope. "And hope does not disappoint us, because God has poured out his love into our hearts" (Rom. 5:5).

My verse cards also challenged me to love the Lord my God with all my heart, soul, and strength (Deut. 6:5). Then I read two of the same promises in different verses: God would instruct me, teach me the way to go, counsel and watch over me, guide me continually, and satisfy my soul in drought (Ps. 32:8; Isa. 58:11).

I wrote in my journal: "It has been a long season of drought without adequate watering of my soul and spirit. The Lord poured out His promises of guidance and love when I felt depressed and hopeless about my future, about giving up working with people I dearly love, leaving work that I enjoy more than any other I have done before."

God had spoken to my heart in the depths of my grief, and I began to feel a new sense of adventure as I waited to see what the Lord had planned for me. I felt humbled and grateful at how He had ministered to me and met my innermost needs with His outpouring of tender promises. For seven days, God comforted me with His assurances of His love and guidance.

And God continued to assure me of His care. I was deeply touched six months later when at the ministry's last chapel we sang the hymn: "All the Way My Savior Leads Me." "Can I doubt His tender mercy, who thru life has been my guide? Heav'nly peace, divinest comfort, Here by faith in Him to dwell! I know what-e'er befall me, Jesus doeth all things well; . . . All the way my Savior leads me; Oh, the fullness of His love!"

Before my final days at the ministry ended, God graciously provided me with an excellent part-time teaching position at the college where I'd been an instructor before. Since then, due to many unexpected health problems and trials, I've realized that the choice God made for my life was the wisest one. God knew what was ahead, as He always does, and His gracious, loving choice was best for me and my family.

Scripture Reading: James 1:22-25

Practicing the Spiritual Life

How does this passage contrast a hearer of the Word with a doer of the Word?

_____

_____

_____

How does the example of looking in a mirror relate to your doing what the Lord desires of you during each moment of a day?

_____

_____

_____

Prayer

Lord, deliver me from the condition of ever hearing but never understanding, ever seeing but never perceiving. May my heart not become calloused so that I hardly hear with my ears and see with my eyes. Jesus, bless my eyes that I may see and my ears that I may hear. May Your Word be sown on good soil in my heart, because I hear and understand it. As I serve You, may my life produce a crop, yielding a hundred, sixty, or thirty times what was sown. (Matt. 13:14-15a, 16, 23 paraphrased)

Prayers, Praises, and Personal Notes

_____

_____

_____

_____

Scripture Reading: Proverbs 4:20–5:2

Practicing the Spiritual Life

Practicing present-moment service to the Lord means that we constantly pay attention to our attitudes and actions. What godly advice can we daily act upon so that we may serve the Lord?

_____

_____

_____

How do those proverbs relate to your own life in regard to listening to God's Spirit and doing what He desires now?

_____

_____

_____

Prayer

Lord, Your precepts are right, giving joy to my heart. Your commands are radiant, giving light to my eyes. Your ordinances are sure and altogether righteous. By them I, Your servant, am warned; in keeping them there is great reward. May the words of my mouth and the meditation of my heart be pleasing in Your sight, O Lord. May I never be lacking in zeal but keep my spiritual fervor, always serving You. (Ps. 19:8, 9b, 11, 14; Rom. 12:11 paraphrased)

Prayers, Praises, and Personal Notes

_____

_____

_____

_____

Scripture Reading: John 13:1-17

Practicing the Spiritual Life
What example did Jesus set as to serving others when He washed the disciples' feet?

_____

_____

_____

Jesus humbly washed the feet of the disciples he loved even though He knew He was going to be betrayed by Judas, denied by Peter, and abandoned by the others. In what ways can you commit yourself to serving others with Christ's humble, loving attitude?

_____

_____

_____

Prayer
Lord, prepare me for works of service, so that the body of Christ may be built up. Teach me how to be as those who are wise and understanding. Help me to show it by my good life, by deeds done in the humility that comes from wisdom. Help me to be ready to do whatever is good, to slander no one, to be peaceable and considerate, and to show true humility toward all people. (Eph. 4:12; James 3:13; Titus 3:1b-2 paraphrased)

Prayers, Praises, and Personal Notes

_____

_____

_____

_____

Scripture Reading: Luke 22:14, 24-27

Practicing the Spiritual Life

During the Last Supper the disciples argued about who would be the greatest. What answer did Jesus give them about how He served others?

_____

_____

_____

Jesus showed us that we serve Him best by having a servant's attitude and doing the most menial tasks. Write down a task you can do with a servant's heart to minister to a specific person. Set a date and time to do that service.

_____

_____

_____

Prayer

Lord, may I be found among those You esteem—by being humble and contrite in spirit and trembling at Your Word. May I serve You with great humility and with tears, even when I am severely tested. May I be known by You for my deeds, my love and faith, my service and perseverance, and for doing more than I am doing now. (Isa. 66:2b; Acts 20:19; Rev. 2:19 paraphrased)

Prayers, Praises, and Personal Notes

_____

_____

_____

_____

_____

Scripture Reading: Luke 9:23-25

Practicing the Spiritual Life

What does taking up our cross mean in regard to serving the Lord?

_____

_____

_____

Is there any duty you're avoiding, but you know God desires you to do it now? If so, commit yourself to deny yourself and do that one duty with a kind and generous attitude. Do you have a task or relationship that you're bitter about? Ask the Lord to forgive you and give you the grace to do what He desires, with a tender heart and loving gladness.

_____

_____

_____

Prayer

O Lord, deliver me from seeking my own good, but let me seek first the good of others. Enable me to devote myself to the service of the saints. Above all, help me to love others deeply, because love covers a multitude of sins. Teach me how to use the gifts I have received to serve others, faithfully administering Your grace in many different ways. When I speak, may I do so as one speaking the very words of God. When I serve, may I do it with the strength You provide, so that in all things You may be praised through Jesus Christ. (1 Cor. 10:24; 16:15b; 1 Peter 4:8, 10-11a paraphrased)

Prayers, Praises, and Personal Notes

_____

_____

_____

Scripture Reading: 1 Samuel 7:3; 12:20-25

Practicing the Spiritual Life
What did Samuel tell the people to remove from their lives?

_____

_____

_____

In what ways does this passage speak to you about the idols you may turn to and serve?

_____

_____

_____

Prayer
Creator of the universe and Maker of all, I will have no other gods before me. I will not make for myself idols in the form of anything in heaven above or on the earth beneath or in the waters below. I will no longer bow down to them or worship them; for You, O Lord my God, are a jealous God. Deliver me from clinging to worthless idols and forfeiting the grace that is mine. By Your mighty power, help me to worship You and serve You only. (Ex. 20:2-4a; Matt. 4:10b paraphrased)

Prayers, Praises, and Personal Notes

_____

_____

_____

_____

_____

_____

Scripture Reading: Joshua 24:1, 14-24

Practicing the Spiritual Life
What does Joshua exhort the people to do in regard to serving the Lord?

_____

_____

_____

What modern time-consuming idols keep you from choosing to serve the Lord with all your heart?

_____

_____

_____

Prayer
One and only God, of what value are idols to me, since I create them? Or a philosophy that teaches me lies? When I make idols, I am trusting in my own creation; when I seek fulfillment in the idols in my life, I am starving my own soul. Can my idols give me guidance? Can my idols give me the love my heart yearns for? Though they may promise everything, they can deliver nothing. How much better for me to get God's wisdom than money, to choose understanding of God's truth rather than the things money can buy. From this day on, I choose Your instruction instead of silver, knowledge rather than choice gold. I choose to serve You faithfully and wholeheartedly, and in doing so, I will fear You. I choose to follow and revere You, keep Your commands and obey them, serve, and hold fast to You. (Hab. 2:18, 19b; Prov. 6:16; 8:10; 1 Chron. 19:3b, 9; Deut. 13:4 paraphrased)

Prayers, Praises, and Personal Notes

_____

_____

_____

WEEK TWELVE

Press On in Painful Circumstances

"Praise be to the God and Father of our Lord Jesus Christ, the Father of compassion and the God of all comfort, who comforts us in all our troubles, so that we can comfort those in any trouble with the comfort we ourselves have received from God."

2 CORINTHIANS 1:3-4

*F*or many years, we've been presented with a Santa Claus Christianity that claims God will magically give us everything we desire. All we have to do is present to God our long wish list and simply believe He'll give us what we ask for. Television shows have also offered a distorted view of life's trials with their thirty- to sixty-minute solutions. Some Christian psychology books and radio and TV programs offer their own easy remedies.

Real life, however, is far different from the patented solutions offered today. God has, in fact, promised suffering as much as He's promised blessings. "Dear friends, do not be surprised at the painful trial you are suffering, as though something strange were happening to you" (1 Peter 4:12). "Even in laughter the heart may ache, and joy may end in grief" (Prov. 14:13). Joys and sorrows are mixed together. And it's the sorrows more than the blessings that challenge and strengthen our faith if we allow them to.

My own spiritual life was born out of pain and delivered to new life through the lengthy labor of suffering. Many seek spiritual strength out of brokenness; others are unable to at all. We may feel as if our faith is strong—until a major problem or heartbreaking disaster whips into our life like a raging firestorm and burns everything to ashes. As we survey the charred rubble of our lives, we feel spiritually incapacitated.

We can't concentrate when we try to read our Bible for comfort. We become so numb that it's difficult to think clearly—let alone pray. We feel distant from God and wonder how He could allow so much to happen to us. And why does He allow the heartache to go on for such a long time?

When heartbreaking trials remain unresolved, no resolution is close at hand, and we recognize there may never be, we're apt to collapse spiritually. This moment of realization is often the most devastating: *My life has been permanently altered by this tragedy, and it will never be the same as it was before.*

As the following real-life proverbs state, the painful truth is that our life may be filled with heartaches that can't be solved with easy answers or simple solutions:

Life can be difficult, painful, and utterly senseless.

Life presents us with challenges and disappointments we'd never choose or ever want to deal with.

Life poses problems we cannot humanly solve.

Life can be as unpredictable as an earthquake that strikes with devastating force.

Life may be unfair, and justice may not be done here on earth.

Life may assault our body and brain with terrible diseases and incredibly painful conditions that modern medicine cannot heal or relieve.

Life may confront us with heartaches and trials that cause us to question our faith.

Those real-life proverbs may sound pessimistic, but anyone who has suffered tough times over many years knows how true they are. Though we may realize that trials are a part of everyday life, it doesn't make them any easier to go through. It matters to us greatly that life can be difficult and painful, changes with little warning, and presents us with problems we cannot solve. When bright hopes burn to ashes, when life crashes in on us with a senseless tragedy and an unfair outcome that makes no sense in human terms, the authenticity of our faith is challenged as never before.

Our spiritual life is either deepened or weakened during those tough times. Over the past eight years alone, our family has passed through many fires; we've felt as if we were deluged by floods of heartaches. In one year our closest friend died at forty-eight. Four months later my husband, Ron, had heart-bypass surgery at the age of fifty-two. My mother-in-law had Alzheimer's disease, cancer, and diabetes and languished in a convalescent home fifteen hundred miles away. Over a period of eight months she lay dying by slow agonizing increments. It was painful being so far away from her during this time. We longed to be near her but couldn't be.

Ron was servicing an auto parts store when the Los Angeles riots spread near the store, and he had to flee. Unfortunately, inner cities are as dangerous as a war combat zone. His life was threatened more than once by drug pushers as he simply went into an auto parts store or warehouse to make sales calls. A godly friend of ours works in the same area and was robbed at knife point.

In the middle of Los Angeles traffic, a man got out of his car, smashed in the back window of Ron's car with his fist, and tried to steal a briefcase on the backseat. Fortunately, Ron drove through a red light and was able to escape.

Ron also has high blood pressure, diabetes, and other serious health problems due in part to his high-stress job. Now because the doctor said his workload has to be reduced, he retired early from the company where he had worked for twenty-three years.

I, too, have struggled with health problems such as sleep apnea, severe night jerking, hearing and balance center disorders. My youngest sister has had two kidney transplants and has broken both of her legs and nearly died several times from sudden diabetic reactions. My oldest sister suffers from brain damage, mental illness, and premature senility due to an aneurysm and brain surgery. Our father passed away last year.

I didn't share this partial list of the many trials we and those we love have experienced as a burden but only as examples that many other Christians can relate to, because so many of us are experiencing similar painful times. I shared them that others might not feel so alone in their own trials. I shared them because, unless we can reconcile ourselves to the endless and often ongoing trials that cause us pain, our faith will give way.

The Truth About Tough Times

We're liable to collapse spiritually if our commitment to Christ is based on what we believe He should do for us or those we love during a trying time. We're apt to give up if our faith is centered on how God should free us from deep trials or change the circumstances or people that we're concerned about. We may turn away from the Lord when our trust in Him is focused on the answers we so desperately want. We're more likely to have a crisis of faith when the final outcome is not only disastrous, but is contrary to everything we believed about God and what we thought He would do.

Three hard facts about tough times need to be accepted if we're going to get past our pain and glorify Christ in the midst of it. First, we will experience the same severe difficulties as everyone else in this world—maybe even more.

Second, we don't always gain relief from pain. The trials we experience may not be resolved and may grow worse. Some afflictions and diseases may last for many years, others for a lifetime. We have friends whose children were born with severe disabilities and medical problems that they will have to cope with their entire lives. Some have family members who have mental illnesses.

Other friends are living with or going through grueling medical treatment for life-threatening diseases.

Several of our Christian friends have children who are alcoholics or drug addicts or who have committed crimes and spent time in jail. These children continue to self-destruct despite the fact that their parents have seen them through rehabilitation programs, sought hours of Christian counseling, prayed faithfully, and done all that they know to do.

Our friends have continued to remain faithful to their Lord, but the enormity of their unrelenting trials is heartbreaking. These parents are devastated, debilitated, and exhausted. They never know when they will receive that next heart-stopping phone call that their children are in serious trouble again.

Third, a crisis of faith often occurs when suffering strikes. One of the greatest threats to maintaining our commitment to Christ is painful trials. That decisive moment when we choose between continuing to trust our Lord or turning away from our faith can come suddenly or over a prolonged period that's been filled with adversities. This crisis can be triggered by something as minor as a simple misunderstanding or as major as the painful death of someone we love.

Working Out Our Faith in Stages

Just as we go through grief-crisis stages when we experience a severe trial or death of a loved one, we go through faith-crisis stages. When we understand those stages, we are better prepared to work through them as we seek our Holy Comforter's healing grace.

The way we find relief from our sorrow and overcome a crisis of faith is by doing the work of grieving. We may not move through this process as quickly as we desire; it takes from one to three years to recover from a major loss. If our trials are ongoing, we may continue to move in and out of the stages of grief and faith-questioning.

Though we may work through those stages and reconcile ourselves to the outcome, some heartaches remain with us for a lifetime. We may be reminded of them at an anniversary, birthday, holiday, or at other moments meaningful only to us. As we open ourselves to Christ's healing love, those times of sorrow diminish.

Here are some principles to help us grow spiritually stronger as we work through our grief and crisis of faith.

Christ's act of reconciliation on the cross redeems our sorrows. Christ suffered for us, and He suffers with us. Our Savior not only died for our sins, He died for our pain. "Suffering makes sense only when we join it to the saving work of Jesus. Apart from Jesus, it is a problem without a solution."[1]

Christ Himself became the solution by redeeming our sorrows. He identifies with our pain and shares our griefs. "He was despised and rejected by men, a man of sorrows, and familiar with suffering. Like one from whom men hide their faces. . . . Surely he took up our infirmities and carried our sorrows" (Isa. 53:3-4a).

Jesus desires to glorify Himself through our afflictions just as He glorified His Father when He died on the cross. Moreover, Christ arose from the grave to bring us out of death into newness of life. That is the hope He has given us, and it is by faith that we, too, will be resurrected from this painful world.

All suffering has spiritual meaning for Christians. As we go through trials, we may seek answers. Why did God allow this heartache? How could God possibly care about us when He let us go through such a senseless tragedy? In wrestling through our questions, it helps to realize that we may never obtain an earthly reason for why we experience such trials.

We find spiritual meaning by comforting others with the same comfort we received from the Lord during our own trials (2 Cor. 1:3-7). We graciously care for those who are hurting even when we still need healing ourselves. The Lord redeems our sorrows by using us to touch the hearts and lives of others with His tender, caring mercy.

Isaiah said, "The Lord God has given me the tongue of those who are taught, that I may know how to sustain with a word him that is weary" (Isa. 50:4-5 RSV). Our caring Counselor will give us the wisdom and words to comfort those who are hurting. Often they simply need us to listen with an empathetic heart. The Lord may even lead us to start or join a special care ministry. Some of the finest ministries were born out of devastating losses and pain.

Trials will strengthen our trust in Christ if we work through our grief and crisis of faith. During the painful stages of grief, we may experience anger and depression, despair and overwhelming sorrow. We may feel numb and in shock, abandoned and isolated. We may ask why. We may try to bargain with God about our trials, promising Him that we'll change or do certain things so that He'll quickly solve the problem or bring healing. As we work through our grief, we may come to the final step of accepting the outcome and reconciling ourselves to the difficult changes in our lives.[2]

As we go through grief stages, we may experience faith-crisis stages. We may feel so shattered we don't see how we can trust the Lord. We may feel spiritually broken and faithless for a period of time.

Old and New Testament accounts are filled with the heart-rending cries of hurting saints. Though the patriarchs, prophets, disciples, and godly women had crises of faith, they still clung to their God, sought His help, and expressed trust in Him. We, too, can find renewed faith when we freely cry out to God. The Psalms are filled with heartfelt expressions of grief that we can offer to the Lord when we're hurting.

Even in our brokenness a tiny seed of confidence in God will grow deeper spiritual roots. We can cling to our Lord no matter how terrible the heartaches or our inability to handle them or our doubts about God and our wavering faith. We can ask God to hold on to us when we can't hold on any longer, and He will.

As we work through a crisis of faith, we may come to accept trials as a part of life. We may come to the place of trusting the Lord to see us through any kind of suffering. We may keep relying on Him even when serious problems remain unresolved. And yet the thought of passing through another heartache is often more than we want to bear. Through God's grace and the exercising of our faith, He enables us to endure unexpected trials that may continue to strike our lives.

Above all, our Redeemer will heal and forgive us. He will empower us to overcome our defeated faith. Our Holy Comforter will tenderly love and care for us. Our mighty God will uphold us and give us the courage we need to endure affliction.

We will safely pass through our crisis of faith and be spiritually renewed as we become reconciled to our Savior and to the outcome of our difficulties and/or ongoing affliction. For "if anyone is in Christ, he is a new creation; the old has gone, the new has come! All this is from God, who reconciled us to himself through Christ and gave us the ministry of reconciliation. We are therefore Christ's ambassadors, as though God were making his appeal through us. We implore you on Christ's behalf: Be reconciled to God" (2 Cor. 5:17-20).

Suffering challenges us to change. Though we may not be able to solve some of our greatest heartaches, we can change our response to trials; our angry, bitter, and unforgiving attitude; our way of handling grief; and our relationship to the Lord.

We can change our response to trials by not denying their reality and by doing the work of grieving. We may try to escape our troubles by denying them, but the pain only becomes worse as our trials escalate and we continue to run away from them. Denial prevents us from seeking godly wisdom and guidance. Denial keeps us from working through our grief. We can change our response to trials by facing them and seeking the help and support we need.

We can change our attitude and feelings about our trials. If we remain angry and unforgiving, we become hard, unkind, and bitter persons. Then we not only hurt ourselves, but our bitterness hurts others.

Some people also cling to their grief and never move beyond their tragic experiences. Because they feel God has abandoned them, they no longer grow in their faith and commitment to Him. They become self-absorbed and obsessed by their pain. They think only of themselves and their own hurts.

If we face our pain during the toughest of trials, work through our grief, and embrace the Lord's healing comfort, we are freed to continue our spiritual journey. We are freed to become caring people of grace, kindness, and love.

We can change our relationship with the Lord by being reconciled to Him in all our afflictions. His Spirit will sustain us as we constantly place ourselves in His presence and maintain an intimate friendship with Him.

Once we do the work of grieving and release our sorrows to our ever-caring Comforter, we will experience His peace that is stronger than our pain. As we open our broken lives to God, He will change us so we become more like Jesus, a compassionate servant of the poor and brokenhearted. Through the ministry of reconciliation, we will console those who are hurting.

Persevering during trials refines our faith and makes us spiritually mature. When our trust is centered on Christ during heartaches, we may become emotionally and physically weaker, but our faith becomes stronger. "Though outwardly we are wasting away, yet inwardly we are being renewed day by day" (2 Cor. 4:16b). Our faith is refined and purified as we glorify Christ in all our afflictions, no matter how trying they may be (1 Peter 1:6-7). As we persevere by faith, we become "mature and complete, not lacking anything" (James 1:4).

Scripture Reading: Ecclesiastes 7:14; 9:1-3a; Lamentations 3:32-33

Practicing the Spiritual Life

Real life can be difficult, painful, and utterly senseless at times. What does God say about good and bad times and the affliction that comes into our lives? What comfort can be drawn from the promises offered in the Lamentations passage?

_____

_____

_____

Have you found it hard to accept that we go through trials that seem unfair and painful? If so, what are those heartaches?

_____

_____

Prayer

Father God, why does the way of the wicked prosper? Why do the faithless live at ease? You have planted them, and they have taken root; they grow and bear fruit. You are always on their lips but far from their hearts. Yet You will bring every deed into judgment, including every hidden thing, whether it is good or evil. Therefore, I will fear You and keep Your commandments, for this is my whole duty. As a father has compassion on his children, have compassion on me because I fear You. Forgive all my sins and heal all my diseases; redeem my life from the pit and crown me with love and compassion. (Jer. 12:1b-2; Eccles. 12:14, 13; Ps. 103:13, 3-4 paraphrased)

Prayers, Praises, and Personal Notes

_____

_____

_____

Scripture Reading: Job 19:5-24

Practicing the Spiritual Life

During difficult trials we may have a crisis of faith and wonder if we will ever gain relief from our sorrows. What did Job say about his great losses and what he endured as a result?

_____

_____

_____

Have you ever felt abandoned by others during a trial as Job did? If so, what similar feelings and experiences did you have?

_____

_____

_____

Prayer

"O my Comforter in sorrow, my heart is faint within me." "You have taken my companions and loved ones from me; the darkness is my closest friend." "I have no refuge; no one cares for my life." In Your great mercy do not put an end to me or abandon me, for You are a gracious and merciful God. Now therefore, great, mighty, and awesome God, You who keep Your covenant of love, do not let all this hardship seem trifling in Your eyes—the hardship that has come upon me. Turn my mourning into gladness; give me comfort and joy instead of sorrow. (Jer. 8:18; Ps. 88:18; 142:4b not paraphrased; Neh. 9:31-32a; Jer. 31:13b paraphrased)

Prayers, Praises, and Personal Notes

_____

_____

_____

Scripture Reading: Job 19:25-27; 42:1-6

Practicing the Spiritual Life

Trials will strengthen our trust in Christ if we work through the stages of grief and crisis of faith. What did Job say to affirm his faith in God?

_____

_____

_____

Write a prayer affirming your trust in God regarding painful heartaches in your life.

_____

_____

_____

Prayer

O my Redeemer, You are strong; the Lord Almighty is Your name. You will vigorously defend my cause so that You may bring rest to me. My eyes are fixed on You, O Sovereign Lord; in You I take refuge. I call on You, for I am poor, and I know You will hear me; You will save me out of all my troubles. You will redeem me, for no one who takes refuge in You will be condemned. "I trust in you, O Lord; I say, 'You are my God.'" "Let your face shine on your servant; save me in your unfailing love." (Jer. 50:34a; Ps. 141:8a; 34:6, 22 paraphrased; Ps. 31:14, 16 not paraphrased)

Prayers, Praises, and Personal Notes

_____

_____

_____

_____

Scripture Reading: 2 Corinthians 4:8-18

Practicing the Spiritual Life

Christ's act of reconciliation on the cross redeems our suffering. How did Paul compare Jesus' death to his own suffering?

_____

_____

_____

What are some of your own attitudes and reactions to unkind treatment and suffering? In what areas of your life do you especially need the Lord's grace to respond as Paul did?

_____

_____

_____

Prayer

O my Savior, You were pierced for my transgressions; You were crushed for my iniquities; the punishment that brings me peace was laid upon You, and by Your wounds I am healed. You were oppressed and afflicted; yet You did not open Your mouth. You were led like a lamb to the slaughter; as a sheep before her shearers is silent, so You did not open Your mouth. You poured out Your life unto death and were numbered with the transgressors. You bore the sins of many and made intercession for the transgressors. Lord Jesus, You gave Yourself for my sins to rescue me from the present evil age, according to Your will, God and Father, to whom be glory forever and ever. Amen. (Isa. 53:5, 7, 12b; Gal. 1:3-4 paraphrased)

Prayers, Praises, and Personal Notes

_____

_____

_____

Scripture Reading: 2 Corinthians 1:3-11; 6:3-10

Practicing the Spiritual Life

All suffering has spiritual meaning for Christians. How did Paul respond to and find spiritual meaning in the hardships he endured?

_____

_____

_____

Write the name of and pray for someone who is in need of comfort. Make a time when you can personally minister to him or her.

_____

_____

_____

Prayer

Heavenly Father, as Your chosen, holy, and dearly beloved child, I will clothe myself with compassion, kindness, humility, gentleness, and patience. I will bear with others and forgive them for the grievances that I have against them. And over all these virtues, I will put on love, which binds them all together in perfect unity. Now send me, tender Shepherd, to bind up the broken-hearted, to proclaim freedom for the captives and release for the prisoners, to comfort all who mourn, and provide for those who grieve—to bestow on them a crown of beauty instead of ashes, the oil of gladness instead of mourning, and a garment of praise instead of a spirit of despair. (Col. 3:12-14; Isa. 61:1b, 2b paraphrased)

Prayers, Praises, and Personal Notes

_____

_____

_____

Scripture Reading: 1 Peter 4:12-19

Practicing the Spiritual Life

Suffering challenges us to change. What should we guard against in times of suffering? How are we to respond to painful trials?

_____

_____

_____

While enduring difficult times, what changes do you need to make in your attitude and life so that you can remain strong in faith?

_____

_____

_____

Prayer

Lord, I humble myself under Your mighty hand that You may lift me up in due time. I cast all my anxiety on You because You care for me. Help me to be self-controlled and alert, for my enemy the devil prowls around like a roaring lion looking for someone to devour. I will resist him, standing firm in the faith, because I know that other Christians throughout the world are undergoing the same kind of sufferings. God of grace, who will call me to Your eternal glory in Christ, after I have suffered a little while, restore me and make me strong, firm, and steadfast. To You be the power forever and ever. Amen. (1 Peter 5:6-11 paraphrased)

Prayers, Praises, and Personal Notes

_____

_____

_____

Scripture Reading: James 1:2-5; 1 Peter 1:6-9

Practicing the Spiritual Life

Persevering during trials refines our faith and makes us spiritually mature. How do the above passages say we're to face trials, and in what ways does suffering develop our faith?

_____

_____

_____

What difficult trials are you experiencing for which you need the Lord's wisdom? Write a prayer asking for strength to persevere by faith.

_____

_____

_____

Prayer

Jesus, I pray that You will know me for my deeds, my hard work, and perseverance—that I persevered and endured hardships for Your name and did not grow weary. For You, O God, test me; You refine me like silver. You know the way I am taking; and when You have finished testing me, I will come forth as gold. Then I will be blessed for persevering under trial, because when I have stood the test, I will receive the crown of life that You have promised to those who love You. (Rev. 2:2a, 3; Ps. 66:10; Job 23:10; James 1:12 paraphrased)

Prayers, Praises, and Personal Notes

_____

_____

_____

PART THREE

Deepening the Spiritual Life

WEEK THIRTEEN

Prepare for a Spiritual Retreat

"Prepare your minds for action;
be self-controlled;
set your hope fully on the grace
to be given you when
Jesus Christ is revealed."

1 PETER 1:13

One weekend morning, I went to the elementary schoolyard at the end of our street for a half-day spiritual retreat. The lush grassy field usually filled with children was now transformed into a bird refuge. Tiny sparrows hopped and skipped across the lawn playing games. Gold-beaked starlings searched the grass for food like children on a treasure hunt.

As I opened my Bible to the selections mentioned in my devotional, I paused to listen to the bird songs, the off-key cawing and melodious chirping. As I turned back to read, this verse was awaiting me, "The birds of the air nest by the waters; they sing among the branches" (Ps. 104:12).

That verse reminded me of Jesus' words, "'Look at the birds of the air; they do not sow or reap or store away in barns, and yet your heavenly Father feeds them. Are you not much more valuable than they? Who of you by worrying can add a single hour to his life?'" (Matt. 6:26-27).

I wondered about my own value in God's eyes, since it had been a particularly difficult week for me. Ron's health problems concerned me. I was experiencing stress-related exhaustion from my ongoing battle with sleep apnea that deprived me of adequate rest, my two-hour daily job commute, long work hours, and some major disappointments. My company was relocating to another state, and I had chosen not to go. I had no idea what I would do in the future and was already feeling the loss of close friends.

As I continued to read about God's care for His helpless creatures, I felt the Lord's reassurance regarding my own sense of helplessness. I watched the carefree antics of the birds and realized how much I needed to release my concerns and worries to the Lord.

Then a monarch butterfly caught my attention. It was drawing nectar from the fragrant honeysuckle vines along the fence. When I went over to see it, the butterfly sailed like a kite around me and over my head and then fluttered back to the flowers. I felt as if I had been given a blessing.

After that I read this passage: "Peace be with you! As the Father has sent me, I am sending you" (John 20:21). The butterfly and verse were a symbol of God's benediction and peace that I needed about the future. For the next few hours the Lord ministered to my concerned heart. I felt renewed and restored when I left my schoolyard sanctuary.

Before and since that time, I have come aside to spend time alone with the Lord often. During my retreats He ministers to me in special ways through His Word; it always speaks to my particular needs and concerns. My caring Shepherd gently guides me, quiets me with His love, and restores my soul (Zeph. 3:17; Ps. 23:3).

Purpose for a Retreat

A spiritual retreat is a gift. It is a present that cannot be bought or sold; it can only be received. The Lord will bestow on us His enriching presence as we read and meditate on Scripture, and pray and listen to His still, small voice. We will receive a deeply satisfying peace and joy, godly wisdom, and understanding "that is more profitable than silver and yields better returns than gold. . . . more precious than rubies" (Prov. 3:14-15).

A retreat is a time to receive and a time to give our love, adoration, and praise to our King of Kings and Lord of Lords. We can give our all to our Savior who has given everything for us. We can surrender our ways, our needs, and our desires to the One who surrendered heaven for earth, who surrendered His life for ours.

A retreat is a time to seek spiritual restoration and renewal. We may also ask for the Lord's guidance regarding a particular need or direction for personal or spiritual goals. We may come desiring a more committed relationship with Him. Or we may come to the retreat without any agenda at all, asking the Holy Spirit to show us God's will.

A retreat is a time to respond to Christ's call to pattern our life after His. We are called to pursue holiness, practice the Lord's presence, and follow Him wherever He leads.

Finding a Quiet Place

Several years ago, I was sitting on the lawn at a conference center. I had planned to spend the weekend having a quiet spiritual retreat. But someone kept gunning a car engine. A chain saw pierced the air with a screaming whine and a final zipping shriek; it was a grating sound like fingernails scratched down a chalkboard. Small groups of people kept wandering through the garden chatting and laughing; they ignored the discreet signs reminding them to reverence the silence.

I had sought a quiet place to read my Bible and write in my journal, so I felt frustrated. Though I didn't say anything, I wanted to shout, "Be quiet! Don't you know you're disturbing me!"

I became increasingly irritated as the rackety noises continued. How would I ever be able to read the Word, spend time in prayer, and listen to the Lord?

I moved several times, sitting beneath a eucalyptus tree, then by the rose garden. Next hidden behind some trees, I found a rock to sit on above the creek. Within minutes a lawn mower sputtered and chugged. After several false starts, it finally started. It clucked, clattered, and snapped as it chucked stones and twigs aside.

I gave up and tramped off to my room overlooking the hills. Silence, utter silence. I had finally found it, but the noise and my frustration had so exhausted me that I slept for two hours.

When I awoke, I thought, *I've wasted the whole day.* But in reality I had not. I had not found a peaceful place to be alone, but the Lord made clear to me that His quiet presence is always with me even when I am deprived of outer silence. I realized that coming aside to seek the Lord was not meant to be a way to escape; it was a way to prepare and return me to the realities of everyday living in a noisy, demanding world.

During another retreat, I expressed these frustrations in my journal: "In listening to God, in trying to listen to the Word, I fight underlying tensions. I'm thirsty. My hands are dry. It's too hot. Then it's too cold. It's too noisy. My stomach gurgles. Anxiety creeps in. My thoughts drift in every direction except where they're supposed to be directed."

During your spiritual retreat you, too, will encounter many different distractions and hindrances. You may struggle because your prayers and the readings seem dry and dull. You may feel as if you are wandering in an arid wilderness with no idea how you will find your way out. You may not feel the Lord's presence and wonder if you ever will.

Those times of dryness strip us of our spiritual self-sufficiency. We may feel so lost we become desperate to find our way home. It is then that we come to a crossroad. One road leads us farther into denial about our misguided attitudes or our inability to surrender our unmet needs or pain to the

Lord. We must also be aware that the enemy will do all that he can to prevent us from strengthening our faith as we seek the Lord.

When we choose the other road, we are willing to be realistic and transparent about our spiritual condition. We are humbled and reminded of our complete dependence upon the Lord for spiritual sustenance. If we keep persevering, keep surrendering and opening ourselves to the Lord and His Word, He will lead us out of the wilderness and satisfy our spiritual thirst.

As we seek to be spiritually renewed, we need to continually release our concerns and distractions to the Lord so that we can listen to His Word. We need to wait upon the Lord rather than demanding that our needs be met. We become rich of faith by submitting ourselves to the poverty of self-denial.

Planning Your Retreat

Since the spiritual retreat, "Promise to Follow the Lord," is the next chapter in this book, you will need to schedule your time for it now. It is a one-day retreat, but plan to take a couple days if you can. Even if you can't spend a day or two, try to set aside at least two hours or more. Or take an hour or two each day and have your retreat over several days.

If weather permits, find a beautiful outdoor setting for your retreat, such as a safe park or beach at a lake, ocean, or river. You may find a conference center that you can go to for the day or weekend. You may be able to stay at a motel, campground, or vacation cabin. Or you may go to a church's sanctuary, quiet room, or gardens.

If you have no other choice, find a place in your own home. Choose a room free of reminders of all the things that need to be done. Turn off your phone. If you have children or other family members, set your retreat time for when they are gone. Or make arrangements for child care.

If possible, have part of your retreat outdoors in a parklike setting. I have spent some of my time at home and some at a nearby park.

When I go on weekend retreats, I start my time early in the morning and continue through the evening. I take breaks for long walks, naps, snacks, and meals. When I stay at a church conference center, I may move to different places outside during the day to have my devotions and then continue my time in my room at night. I also go to the chapel or sanctuary to worship the Lord. I may read or quietly sing selections in the hymnbook.

Wherever you choose to go, find a safe and restful place. I've chosen a couple of places that turned out to be too distracting or disturbing and had to leave them. Now I carefully choose the places that I go to for a retreat.

You will need to bring your Bible and several pens. Though lined spaces to write on are provided in the retreat guide, you may also want to use a journal or notebook paper and index cards.

Plan to wear comfortable casual clothes and walking shoes. Have light and heavier clothing available in case the weather turns too hot or cold. If you go outdoors, you may need a hat, sun or mosquito protective lotion, folding lawn chair, or blanket. It's also essential that you have access to a restroom.

Prepare food for your retreat ahead of time. Plan to eat lightly, and stay away from high-sugar foods that cause drowsiness. You may want to take a cooler with sandwiches, fruit, and hot or cold drinks.

During the retreat, your body will whine and cry for food, water, and restroom breaks. Try to gain a balance between meeting those needs and refusing those demands; you need to overcome them so you can concentrate on your quiet time with the Lord.

You may want to fast during the retreat if your health and your doctor permits it. If you haven't fasted before, don't try a lengthy one. I have done partial fasts, such as going without a single meal. I may go without breakfast and lunch and then have a light dinner. Since I have low blood sugar, I always drink fruit and vegetable juices, hot broths, and plenty of water. I have to be careful about fasting, but I find that it is spiritually purifying.

How does fasting benefit our spiritual life? "Fasting is the act of temporarily giving up something that is very important to us in order that we may use the time normally given to that thing for prayer and reflect upon the pain of the temporary 'sacrifice' to better understand the mystery and meaning of Christ's passion and sacrifice for us. Our prayers for others can be greatly strengthened by fasting."[1] This kind of praying calls for self-crucifixion. You will find yourself in a brutal warfare with fleshly urgencies. You will constantly battle your mental, emotional, and physical cravings.

You may be consumed with a ravenous hunger for food or a desire for your usual schedule, habits, and other activities. During a retreat, I also fast from doing hobbies, listening to the radio, watching television, and reading newspapers and periodicals.

We overcome our urgent cravings by constantly bringing our thoughts back to God and presenting our supplications for others before Him. If we keep telling ourselves not to think about them, our cravings only become stronger.

If you're a clock-watcher like me, try to relax and don't be concerned about the time. During my first retreats, I felt pressed to keep a schedule and complete the devotional materials. Now I take my time and follow the retreat plan at my own pace. If I don't finish it, I may continue the retreat as part of my devotional time during the following week.

After you have completed your retreat, you may want to set a date on your calendar to reread your retreat responses to see where you are in regard to any commitments you might have made or what prayers might have been answered. You may also want to schedule another retreat. Some people have monthly retreats; others go on retreat every three to four months or once or twice a year. A two- or three-hour mini-retreat is also spiritually refreshing.

Preparing for a Retreat

This week's devotionals are the foundation you will be laying for the spiritual sanctuary you will be building during your retreat. The more prepared you are, the more you will be spiritually renewed—the more Christ will be able to transform you into His image.

Here are the parts of the retreat (italics) with suggestions to help you know what to expect and how to make it more meaningful.

The retreat is divided into three parts: *Morning Quiet Time, Midday,* and *Afternoon Quiet Time.* Begin your retreat at an hour best suited for you. Some people are early risers, others late.

Recreation. Plan to walk at the beginning and during your retreat. Light exercise will stimulate your system and help you think more clearly during the longer periods of sitting. At anytime during the retreat feel free to move around, get a snack, or have a meal.

Hymn to Sing or Reflect On. The hymns give you the opportunity to worship the Lord in song. If you do not know them, reflect on the words, on what they mean to you and your spiritual life.

Respond. Lined spaces are included for this part of the retreat so you can write your responses to the hymns and a time of quiet listening.

Scripture Reading, Practicing the Spiritual Life, and Prayer. These familiar sections from the previous weeks' devotionals are included in the retreat.

Quiet Listening. This is a time to simply listen and wait upon the Lord. It's a time to think about the hymns, the Word, and what God might be wanting to say to you through them. You will begin to hear and understand His Word and His desires for your life as you quietly listen. "Do not fear the solitude and silence of retreat. They can be the friends that reveal the presence of God."[2]

Be prepared to wrestle with cravings, distractions, and unruly thoughts. You may want to close your eyes to help you focus on hearing, or you may want to watch and listen if you're outdoors. Rest in the Lord as you watch His smallest of creatures and enjoy the trees, flowers, or a lake, ocean, or stream. Wait quietly. Wait expectantly. "Wait for the Lord; be strong and take heart and wait for the Lord" (Ps. 27:14).

Scripture Reading: Luke 10:38-41

Practicing the Spiritual Life

We prepare for our retreat by releasing our concerns and distractions to the Lord. What distracted Martha, and what did she miss as a result?

_____

_____

_____

Do you have any anxieties or worries about tasks that might be left undone? What expectations do you have for the spiritual retreat? What do you desire to gain from sitting at Jesus' feet?

_____

_____

_____

Prayer

O Prince of Peace, my anxious heart weighs me down. Help me to banish anxiety from my heart and cast off the troubles of my body. Deliver me from worrying about tomorrow, for tomorrow will worry about itself. Each day has enough trouble of its own. When anxiety is great within me, may Your consolation bring joy to my soul. May Your grace and peace be with me. (Prov. 12:25; Matt. 6:34; Ps. 94:19; Eccles. 11:10a; Col. 1:2 paraphrased)

Prayers, Praises, and Personal Notes

_____

_____

_____

_____

_____

Scripture Reading: 1 Peter 1:13-16

Practicing the Spiritual Life

A spiritual retreat is a time to pursue holiness. In what ways are we to prepare ourselves to be holy as Christ is holy?

_____

_____

_____

Are there any spiritual disciplines that you would like to begin or strengthen during this time?

_____

_____

_____

Prayer

Almighty God, I will put on Your full armor so that I can take my stand against the devil's schemes. For my struggle is not against flesh and blood but against the rulers, against the authorities, against the powers of this dark world, and against the spiritual forces of evil in the heavenly realms. Therefore, I will put on Your full armor, so that when the day of evil comes, I may be able to stand my ground, and after I have done everything, to stand. I will stand firm then with the belt of truth buckled around my waist, with the breastplate of righteousness in place, and with my feet fitted with the readiness that comes from the Gospel of peace. In addition to all this, I will take up the shield of faith, with which I can extinguish all the flaming arrows of the evil one. I will take the helmet of salvation and the sword of the Spirit, which is the Word of God. (Eph. 6:11-17 paraphrased)

Prayers, Praises, and Personal Notes

_____

_____

_____

Scripture Reading: 2 Timothy 2:19-22

Practicing the Spiritual Life
A retreat is a time to give ourselves to the Lord. How can we become instruments for His use?

_____

_____

_____

Are there any preparations that you need to make for the retreat? In what ways do you need to purify your life so you can be used by the Lord?

_____

_____

_____

Prayer
Most holy Lord, whatever is true, whatever is noble, whatever is admirable— if anything is excellent or praiseworthy—I will think about such things. Whatever I have learned or received or heard from those who are godly or whatever I have seen in them, I will put into practice. In the same way, I will let my light shine before others that they may see my good deeds and praise You, Father in heaven. Now may the good work I do be produced by faith, my labor be prompted by love, and my endurance inspired by my hope in You, Lord Jesus Christ. (Phil. 4:8-9a; Matt. 5:16; 1 Thess. 1:3 paraphrased)

Prayers, Praises, and Personal Notes

_____

_____

_____

_____

Scripture Reading: Isaiah 55:6-7

Practicing the Spiritual Life

A retreat is a time to seek spiritual restoration and renewal. How are we to seek the Lord?

_____

_____

_____

Write a prayer asking the Lord to free you from any sins that might hinder you from seeking Him during the retreat.

_____

_____

_____

Prayer

Lord, the Son of Righteousness, You have declared, "Your wickedness will punish you; your backsliding will rebuke you." I will consider and realize how evil and bitter it is for me if I forsake You and have no awe of You, O Lord my God. For You love those who love You; those who seek You will find You. I will listen to You, pursue righteousness, and seek You. I will seek You and rejoice; I will be glad in You, for I love your salvation, and I will always say, "Let God be exalted!" (Jer. 2:19; Prov. 8:17; Ps. 70:4 paraphrased)

Prayers, Praises, and Personal Notes

_____

_____

_____

_____

_____

Scripture Reading: Isaiah 55:8-9

Practicing the Spiritual Life

A retreat is a time to respond to the Lord and surrender our ways and needs to Him. What does the Lord say about His ways compared to ours?

_____

_____

_____

Are there any of your thoughts or ways that you need to surrender to the Lord as you prepare for this retreat?

_____

_____

_____

Prayer

"You know me, O Lord; you see me and test my thoughts about You." You know my thoughts; You know when they are futile. Help me to be a prudent person who gives thought to my steps. For righteousness goes before You, O Holy God, and prepares the way for Your steps. Your way is perfect. You are righteous in all Your ways and loving toward all You have made. Everything You do is right, and all Your ways are just. Lord Almighty, arm me with strength and make my way perfect. (Jer. 12:3a not paraphrased; Ps. 94:11; Prov. 14:15; Ps. 85:13; 145:17; Dan. 4:37b; Ps. 18:32 paraphrased)

Prayers, Praises, and Personal Notes

_____

_____

_____

_____

Scripture Reading: Isaiah 55:10-11

Practicing the Spiritual Life

A retreat is a time to read and meditate on Scripture. What does this passage say about God's Word?

_____

_____

_____

Write a prayer asking the Lord to prepare your heart through the Word.

_____

_____

_____

Prayer

Jesus, You are the Farmer who sows the Word. And I am like seed along the path where the Word is sown. Deliver me from Satan who will try to come and snatch away the Word that was sown in me. May I not be like seed sown on rocky places, hearing the Word and at once receiving it with joy. But since it has no root, it lasts only a short time. When trouble or persecution comes because of the Word, deliver me from quickly falling away. May I not be like seed sown among thorns, hearing the Word; but the worries of this life, the deceitfulness of wealth, and the desires for other things come in and choke the Word, making it unfruitful in me. Instead may I be like seed sown on good soil, hearing the Word, accepting it, and producing a crop—thirty, sixty, or even a hundred times what was sown. (Matt. 13:18; Mark 4:14-20 paraphrased)

Prayers, Praises, and Personal Notes

_____

_____

_____

Scripture Reading: Isaiah 55:12-13

Practicing the Spiritual Life

A retreat is a time to freely give our love, adoration, and praise to our King of Kings and Lord of Lords. How does joyous praise and singing honor the Lord?

_____

_____

_____

Record praises to the Lord for the ways He has been ministering to you this week and for how He will spiritually renew you during your retreat.

_____

_____

_____

Prayer

O joyous One, my mouth is filled with laughter, my tongue with songs of joy. I will enter Zion with singing; everlasting joy will crown my head. Gladness and joy will overtake me, and sorrow and sighing will flee away. I delight greatly in You, Lord of glory; my soul rejoices in You, my God and Savior. For You have clothed me with garments of salvation and arrayed me in a robe of righteousness, as a bridegroom adorns his head like a priest and as a bride adorns herself with jewels. For as the soil makes the sprout come up and a garden causes seeds to grow, so You, Sovereign Lord, will make righteousness and praise spring up before all nations. (Ps. 126:2; Isa. 35:10; 61:10-11 paraphrased)

Prayers, Praises, and Personal Notes

_____

_____

_____

WEEK FOURTEEN

Promise to Follow the Lord

"'I am the light of the world.
Whoever follows me will
never walk in darkness,
but will have the light of life.'"

JOHN 8:12

SPIRITUAL RETREAT GUIDE

*R*ead the hymns and Scripture passages slowly; reflect on how the words relate to your own life and needs. Ask the Spirit of God to show you His thoughts and ways. Seek the Lord's will and ask Him to strengthen you to follow His guidance. Respond to Him with an open heart and open mind.

Ask Jesus to help you clearly hear His truth as you are praying, reading the selections, and writing your responses. Pour out your prayers to the Lord as if He is your dearest friend, the one you love more than any others.

When your thoughts wander, go back and read the hymns or verses again. Ask the Lord to help you focus on the meaning of the passages and to listen with purity of heart.

Write verses that especially speak to your concerns and needs on index cards (include the date). Later, when you reread those Scriptures and your retreat notes, you may find that they prepared you for an answer to prayer and showed how God would work.

Prepare for the Retreat

Date _____

Do you have any needs, obligations, or worries that are concerning you now? If so, write them down and release them to the Lord.

_____

_____

_____

What are the desires of your heart for this time with the Lord?

_____

_____

_____

Morning Quiet Time

Lord Jesus, my feet will closely follow Your steps;
I will keep Your way without turning aside.
I will not depart from the commands of Your lips;
I will treasure the words of Your mouth more than my daily bread.

JOB 23:11-12 (paraphrased)

Recreation (10 to 20 minutes)

Walk slowly and consistently. Release your concerns and burdens to the Lord. Ask Him to speak to you according to the desires of His heart for your life. You may want to write the above passage on an index card. As you walk, carry the card, read and reflect on the verses, and pray for help to follow the Lord's steps.

Read and Respond

Find a quiet place for your time with the Lord. Write your responses as you feel the need and after any of the following "Scripture Readings," "Hymns to Sing or Reflect On," and "Quiet Listening."

Scripture Reading: Matthew 19:16-29

Practicing the Spiritual Life

What kept the young man from following Jesus?

_____

_____

_____

Is anything keeping you from following and serving Jesus?

_____

_____

_____

WHERE HE LEADS ME

1. I can hear my Savior calling,
I can hear my Savior calling,
I can hear my Savior calling,
"Take thy cross and follow, follow Me."

Chorus:

Where He leads me I will follow,
Where He leads me I will follow,
Where He leads me I will follow,
I'll go with Him, with Him all the way.

2. I'll go with Him thru the garden,
I'll go with Him thru the garden,
I'll go with Him thru the garden,
I'll go with Him, with Him all the way.

4. He will give me grace and glory,
He will give me grace and glory,
He will give me grace and glory,
And go with me, with me all the way.[1]

Respond

When Jesus went to the Garden of Gethsemane, "he fell with his face to the ground and prayed, 'My Father, if it is possible, may this cup be taken from me. Yet not as I will, but as you will'" (Matt. 26:39). In what areas of your life do you need to surrender your will to the Lord in order to do His will and serve Him?

_____

_____

_____

_____

_____

Prayer

Jesus, You said that "unless a kernel of wheat falls to the ground and dies, it remains only a single seed. But if it dies, it produces many seeds." If I love my life, I will lose it, but if I hate my life in this world, I will keep it for eternal life. To serve You, I must follow You; and where You are, I, your servant, must also be. For You will honor me for serving You. (John 12:24-27 paraphrased)

Quiet Listening (15 to 30 minutes)

As you quiet your thoughts before the Lord, you will battle both outward and inward distractions. Keep persevering; keep bringing your thoughts back to God. Ask Him to help you hear Him and to overcome any thoughts that are not from Him. Then record your responses, confess sins and struggles, and note spiritual insights.

> *"Speak, Lord, for your servant is listening."*
>
> 1 SAMUEL 3:9B

Respond

_____

_____

_____

Recreation and Refreshment

Take a brief walk and have a light snack if you need to.

Scripture Reading: Luke 9:21-26

Practicing the Spiritual Life

What are the costs of following Jesus?

_____

_____

_____

What concerns or fears do you have about the sacrifices you may need to make to follow Jesus?

_____

_____

_____

Hymn to Sing or Reflect On

JESUS, I MY CROSS HAVE TAKEN

1. Jesus, I my cross have taken, All to leave and follow Thee;
Destitute, despised, forsaken— Thou from hence my all shalt be.
Perish ev'ry fond ambition— All I've sought and hoped and known!
Yet how rich is my condition— God and heav'n are still my own!

2. Let the world despise and leave me— They have left my Savior too;
Human hearts and looks deceive me— Thou art not, like man, untrue.
And while Thou shalt smile upon me, God of wisdom, love, and might,
Foes may hate, and friends may shun me— Show Thy face, and all is bright!

3. Hasten on from grace to glory, Armed by faith and winged by prayer;
Heav'ns eternal day's before me— God's own hand shall guide me there.
Soon shall close my earthly mission, Swift shall pass my pilgrim days;
Hope shall change to glad fruition, Faith to sight, and prayer to praise! [2]

Respond

Are there any ambitions, dreams, or desires that you feel Jesus is asking you to let go of and leave behind in order to take up His cross and follow Him?

_____

_____

_____

_____

_____

Prayer

Jesus, I have been crucified with You, and I no longer live, but You live in me. The life I live in my body, I live by faith in You, Son of God, who loved me and gave Yourself for me. For if I died with You, I will also live with You; if I endure, I will also reign with You. If I suffer for doing right and I endure it, this is well pleasing to You, Lord. For even to this I was called—it is inseparable from my vocation. For You also suffered for me, leaving me Your personal example, that I should follow in Your footsteps. Now may I never boast except in Your cross, Lord Jesus Christ, through which the world has been crucified to me and I to the world. (Gal. 2:20; 2 Tim. 2:11-12a; 1 Peter 2:20b-21 AMP; Gal. 6:14 paraphrased)

Quiet Listening (15 to 30 minutes)

I will be still before the Lord.

ZECHARIAH 2:13A (paraphrased)

Respond

_____

_____

_____

_____

_____

_____

_____

_____

_____

_____

MIDDAY

Refreshment, Recreation and Rest (30 minutes to 1 hour)

Have lunch, walk, and rest. Relax and enjoy this break. Make it a time of praise, thanksgiving, and worship.

AFTERNOON QUIET TIME

Scripture Reading: Matthew 4:18-22

Practicing the Spiritual Life

How did Simon, Andrew, James, and John respond to Jesus' call to follow Him? What did Jesus call them to do?

_____

_____

_____

_____

_____

What is the Lord calling you to do for Him?

_____

_____

_____

_____

_____

_____

_____

_____

_____

I'LL GO WHERE YOU WANT ME TO GO

1. It may not be on the mountain's height
Or over the stormy sea,
It may not be at the battle's front
My Lord will have need of me;
But if by a still, small voice He calls
To paths I do not know,
I'll answer, dear Lord, with my hand in Thine,
I'll go where You want me to go.
Chorus:

I'll go where You want me to go, dear Lord,
O'er mountain or plain or sea;
I'll say what You want me to say, dear Lord,
I'll be what You want me to be.

2. Perhaps today there are loving words
Which Jesus would have me speak,
There may be now, in the paths of sin,
Some wand'rer whom I should seek;
O Savior, if Thou wilt be my Guide,
Tho dark and rugged the way,
My voice shall echo the message sweet,
I'll say what You want me to say.

3. There's surely somewhere a lowly place
In earth's harvest fields so wide,
Where I may labor thru life's short day
For Jesus the Crucified;
So, trusting my all unto Thy care—
I know Thou lovest me—
I'll do Thy will with a heart sincere,
I'll be what You want me to be.[3]

Respond

In what ways did this hymn speak to you about going where the Lord wants you to go to serve others?

_____

_____

_____

_____

_____

Prayer

Lord, I will hold fast to You and will not cease to follow You; I will keep Your commands that You have given. I will fear You and serve You with all faithfulness. I will serve You faithfully and wholeheartedly in reverence. Lord, God of my Fathers, as long as I live, I will not fail to follow You. I will go forth in Your strength and proclaim Your mighty acts with a sincere heart. (2 Kings 18:6; Josh. 24:14a; 2 Chron. 19:24; 34:33b; Psalm 71:16a paraphrased)

Quiet Listening (15 to 30 minutes)

> _I love You, Lord God. I will listen to Your voice_
> _and hold fast to You. For You are my life._
>
> DEUTERONOMY 30:20A (paraphrased)

Respond

_____

_____

_____

_____

_____

_____

Recreation and Refreshment

Take a brief walk and have a light snack if you need to.

Review and Respond

Read over what you've written in your responses. Has the Lord guided you in a special way through the Scriptures, hymns, retreat setting, or during your prayers and quiet listening? If so, what do you feel the Lord has impressed on your heart and mind?

_____

_____

_____

_____

_____

How has the Lord ministered to you and met your own personal needs and concerns?

_____

_____

_____

_____

_____

Are there any commitments that you would like to make to the Lord? If so, set a specific time period to meet those commitments.

_____

_____

_____

_____

_____

_____

In the days ahead, what do you desire the Lord to do in your life as you follow Him and serve others?

_____

_____

_____

> *"You are my portion, O Lord;*
> *I have promised to obey your words.*
> *I have sought your face with all my heart;*
> *be gracious to me according to your promise.*
> *I have considered my ways and have turned my steps*
> *to your statutes. I will hasten and not delay*
> *to obey your commands. All your words are true;*
> *all your righteous laws are eternal.*
> *Praise be to the Lord forever! Amen and Amen."*

PSALM 119:57-60, 160; 89:52

Plans for a Small Group Study and Spiritual Retreat

A Woman's Walk with God was written to strengthen our faith. The purpose of this book is to help us discover the spiritual life, develop the disciplined life, and deepen our devotional life. It was designed to offer creative ways to have devotions and to broaden our view of how we grow spiritually. This devotional offers us grace rather than guilt and encourages us to discover the joys of a more committed friendship with our Lord.

Starting a Small Group

Although this devotional book was written for individuals, it also works well with small groups and with women of all ages meeting together. The women in my classes ranged from their twenties to their seventies.

Check with potential class members to see what day of the week would be the best for them to meet. I have held classes during the church school hour and on a week night. The thirteen weeks of devotional studies make it ideal for a quarterly class schedule. During the fourteenth week the group will have a spiritual retreat that you will need to plan for and schedule when you start the class.

Set a time schedule. You may find that meeting for an hour is too brief.

Ninety minutes for the study and light refreshments is ideal. This creates an informal atmosphere and allows for more personal sharing and prayer time.

Here's an example of a ninety-minute session: Spend ten minutes quietly listening to and singing hymns and/or worship songs, twenty minutes discussing the introductory chapter, thirty minutes on the devotionals, twenty minutes for prayer, and ten minutes for refreshments and fellowship.

Find a place for the class to meet. A home may be more comfortable than a classroom for this kind of devotional study. But if you meet in a classroom and the setting is less than ideal, you can still set the right tone. Our class met in the preschoolers' room. Every week I put the toys away and set up a portable screen to block off part of the play area. I decorated a small table with either a crocheted or lace cloth, lighted candles, and flowers or other simple decorations that correlated with the theme of the study.

A week before the first meeting, make sure class members have this book. Ask them to read and do the devotionals for Week One, "Prepare to Rest." That way you will be able to follow the format of the book and begin group discussion right away.

Leader Preparation

Plan to cover the weekly chapters in one session. The group will be completing the introductory chapter and seven days of devotionals in preparation for the upcoming class.

Read all the chapters before the first class starts. That way you will know what is covered in the book and will be better prepared to guide the class. When people ask questions about a future topic, you can let them know that the subject will be covered later.

As you read over the chapter and do the devotions each week, highlight or underline the main points and spiritual applications. Since there is usually not enough time to cover all seven devotionals during class, decide which statements or questions from "Practicing the Spiritual Life" you will use for discussion.

Begin incorporating the spiritual disciplines and suggestions for how to have devotions into your own life. Make note of the ways the Lord ministers to you as you read the chapter and do the devotions. Then share with the class how you were ministered to and give personal examples of how the Lord has helped you. The more committed you are to strengthen your spiritual life, the more you will encourage others in the group to do the same.

At the same time, be transparent about your own spiritual struggles. If you present yourself as the perfect Christian, class members will feel imperfect and inferior.

Prayer is an essential part of your preparation. Pray for class members, and let them know you are doing so. Pray that they will grow in Christ and be strengthened in their faith and commitment to Him. Pray for the class sessions, that the Lord will have His hand on them and lead you in guiding the discussion. Pray for the Holy Spirit's guidance and wisdom. Pray that your walk with Christ will be strengthened and ask for help to practice the spiritual disciplines.

Prepare visual aids to make the class more interesting and to help members gain information according to their learning styles. Write a brief outline of the main points of the chapter on a chalk or marker board or use an easel with large sheets of paper. This will give the class direction and help you keep the discussion on track.

Small Group Guidelines

Ask people to bring their Bibles, this devotional book, and a couple of pens. Though some people may not feel comfortable writing in a published book, encourage them to freely write down their answers, prayers, and personal notes. They may also want to use notebook paper or a journal to write additional comments, verses, or spiritual insights.

Have the class sit in a circle, semicircle, or around a table. This is more personal and facilitates discussion because people are facing each other and don't have to look around to see who is speaking. People who are hard of hearing read lips and facial expressions to help them hear better, so they especially need to see others who speak.

If the class is large, divide it into groups of four to eight people. Either choose discussion leaders or ask the groups to choose their own. Many people feel more comfortable sharing when there are fewer members. This also allows them to participate more, and they can get to know each other in a more personal way.

Each week remind the group to read the chapter and complete the devotionals for the next session. Lack of preparation limits the discussion, because fewer people are ready to share. The more people who prepare, the greater the benefit for the entire group and for themselves as well.

Encourage the group to underline and reflect on passages in the text that were especially meaningful to them. Ask them to return to class ready to share spiritual insights and/or questions. This will make the class more interesting and will be an incentive for the other members.

Motivate the class to complete the devotionals for the next week by giving an assignment from one of the questions in "Practicing the Spiritual Life."

Class Session Plans

Provide name tags for the first couple of meetings. Have the women introduce themselves. Keep introductions brief by asking the members to tell one thing about themselves. Or ask them to say what they desire to gain from the devotional study. This is an excellent way to discover what the group members' expectations are regarding the study.

Be sure to start class on time. The later you start, the later people will come. Those who are early or on time will become frustrated by the delay.

Warmly welcome people as they come into the classroom. You may want to ask a friendly person to greet people as they arrive. When new members join the class, take a few minutes for introductions.

Set a devotional atmosphere. I used a cassette recorder and softly played Christian music as members arrived. We spent the first five minutes quietly listening to hymns and worship songs. This provided a peaceful setting that helped the people release their tensions and gave them an opportunity to pray, worship, and spiritually prepare themselves.

The weekly title page has a Scripture passage that group members may use for memorization. Memorization is difficult for some people, so be careful not to embarrass those who don't learn the verses. Other people may want to memorize some of the verses but not all of them. You may want to say the verses aloud together before you begin discussion.

As the teacher or leader, explain to the group that the devotional study is for people in different stages of spiritual growth, from new believers to the mature in faith. Some may feel embarrassed because they don't have devotions or feel guilty about the amount of time they spend with the Lord. Others may try to have devotions but can't keep their thoughts focused during their time with the Lord, or they may come away feeling dry or dissatisfied. This class is for all seekers who desire to grow in their faith.

Here is a format that you may want to follow for the class:

Open class with prayer and a hymn or worship songs that correlate with the theme of the study. If you don't have someone who can play the piano or guitar, use cassette tapes you can sing along with, or sing without an instrument.

If you have one small group, discuss together the highlights of the chapter and the questions or statements from "Practicing the Spiritual Life." If the class is large, you may want to briefly share highlights from the introductory chapter, giving personal illustrations from your own spiritual journey. Then the class can go to their small groups to discuss the devotionals.

Close in prayer, asking people to briefly share prayer requests. Encourage the group to pray for each other during the week. They may write prayer requests in their books under "Prayers, Praises, and Personal Notes" or on the lined spaces at the end of the chapters.

Have light refreshments after the session. This allows people time to share informally. This will also give some people the opportunity to ask you questions that they didn't feel comfortable discussing with the group. They may need to share personal concerns or burdens with you. If you have group leaders, ask them to be available to the people in their groups during this time.

Be mindful that many people are busy and work long hours, so it is important to begin and end on time as much as possible. Those who want to stay for refreshments will, and those who need to leave will feel free to go.

Group Discussion Guidelines

Open discussion and group participation are the best methods for using this devotional material. People remember more of what they do and say, so keep lectures to a minimum. Be a facilitator who guides the discussion and keeps the class on track and on schedule.

Be relaxed, and the class will feel more at ease. This doesn't mean that the class is unstructured. Maintain an informal friendly manner while guiding the discussion in an orderly way.

Involve as many people as possible. You may want to go around the group, asking each member to answer different questions or contribute a comment. People who don't feel comfortable entering into the discussion may be willing to read Scripture aloud.

When you ask a question, allow people enough time to answer. If you don't get a response, restate the question in another way. Or call on someone that you know will feel comfortable answering.

Once a question has been discussed, give a brief summary of the answers that have been offered by the group.

Ask the group to share personal examples of what they learned in the devotional study or how God has been working in their lives and changing them. The more people see that the Lord can change their lives and others, the more enthusiastic they will be about growing in their faith and commitment to Him.

Stress confidentiality. Ask the group not to discuss with people outside the class personal information shared by members.

Some people may feel uncomfortable answering the personal questions about their spiritual life. Others will gladly volunteer. Respect people's comfort level.

The group will gain more from the class if you do all that you can to keep the discussion balanced. When people get off onto different tangents, bring the discussion back to the main topic as quickly as possible.

Thank people for their answers regardless of how these relate to the subject. When an answer is incorrect, don't embarrass the person by correcting him or her. Instead ask other group members to contribute their answers.

Some people consistently offer answers or share personal needs totally unrelated to the subject. Remind them that they need to focus on the topic of discussion.

Keep more vocal members from dominating the group. When a person keeps talking without pausing, you may have to interrupt him or her. You might say something like this, "Excuse me, we appreciate what you have to say, but we need to give others an opportunity to share." Then ask another person to contribute an answer. If certain members continue monopolizing the discussion, you may need to talk to them privately.

Everyone is in a different place spiritually. Some of the group members will be mature; others will be new believers. Some will be committed to growing in their faith; others will have little desire to grow at all. Some people have been Christians for many years but have not grown in their faith. They may be defensive, embarrassed, or unaware of their spiritual condition. Still others may be angry, bitter, and/or rebellious due to a painful church experience.

Set an open, accepting tone by constantly affirming those who may feel that they aren't as spiritual as others. Be gracious and kind to those who are hurting deeply and/or questioning their faith. Be patient and loving with those who may have bitter attitudes. Pray for the transforming power of the Holy Spirit to work in all of your lives.

Most people feel inferior around Christians who seem to have all the correct answers and can quote the right verse for every difficulty. They may also spiritualize their problems and appear to handle their lives in a perfect manner no matter how many trials they face.

If people feel that they are being judged or that they do not measure up to the standards of perfect Christians, they will not return to the group. Privately remind Christians who act in a spiritually superior or judgmental way that we need to humbly encourage and build others up.

We all need the assurance that our Lord loves us with a love that is beyond our comprehension. Because He loves us so much, He will always be available to support and strengthen us as we grow in Him, and we need to do the same for each other.

The Devotional Retreat

A retreat for spiritual renewal may also be called a silent retreat, because the people will be spending time alone with the Lord without talking to each other. Silence is maintained until the early afternoon when the group gathers for sharing, worship, communion, and fellowship. Though the idea of being with people without speaking may seem difficult, the group will discover that this time alone with the Lord will be spiritually renewing.

When I first mentioned to our class that we would be spending a day together without talking, they couldn't imagine that it would be possible. At the end of the retreat, however, they felt that the time had gone by too quickly and were already talking about having another one.

Group members will need reassurance, because they will feel uncomfortable about not speaking to the others. A silent devotional retreat has an added dimension that you may miss when you have a retreat alone. You feel the prayers and the presence of Lord when many are gathered together. You feel spiritually strengthened and uplifted by the others even though you aren't talking with them.

Group Retreat Plans

Choose a quiet, peaceful place for the retreat. We had a one-day retreat at a home with a lovely garden and pool. A small park was a block away. Some people sat by the pool, others in the front yard, while others went to the park. If you have a conference center nearby, you may be able to use their grounds for a day.

Set a day and time for the retreat. We had ours on a Saturday from 9:30 A.M. to 3:30 P.M. Depending on your group, you may want to start earlier and/or go later in the day.

Follow the suggestions in Week Thirteen on preparing for the retreat. Make a sign-up sheet for people to help with setup and cleanup and to bring food, drinks, paper plates, cups, napkins, and bags of ice. We kept the food simple. We brought coolers with ice that held containers of juice and milk. We also had coffee, muffins, and fresh fruit available throughout the day for snacks. We had sandwiches, carrot and celery sticks, corn and potato chips, ice tea, and sodas for lunch. For our afternoon fellowship time we had a light dessert.

We didn't have the morning snack or lunch together. Some people set up the snack while others laid out the food for lunch. Others took care of cleaning up. We maintained our time of silence during this time and until we met for worship and fellowship.

Use the Week Fourteen, "Promise to Follow the Lord," retreat and schedule with the following additions. Have a closing worship and Communion service and a fellowship time with a snack. Sing hymns and worship songs during the worship time. Ask people to share how the Lord ministered to them during the retreat. Then close with Communion.

Our retreat was a spiritually renewing experience. For me, it was life-changing as I sat at Jesus' feet and felt His powerful presence in the love and prayers of my friends. The Lord sent me out from that time with a greater desire to follow Him.

It is my prayer that as you go forth to comfort, minister, and serve others, you may be filled with joyous praise as you watch with wonder the amazing work of the Lord in your life and the lives of others.

NOTES

WEEK FIVE: PUT YOUR SPIRITUAL JOURNEY IN A DEVOTIONAL JOURNAL

1. Jan Johnson, *Journeying Through the Days 1995: A Calendar & Journal for Personal Reflection* (Nashville: The Upper Room, 1994).
2. Rueben P. Job, *Journeying Through the Days 1994: A Calendar & Journal for Personal Reflection* (Nashville: The Upper Room, 1993).
3. Johnson, *Journeying Through the Days 1995.*
4. Ibid.

WEEK SIX: PRACTICE THE SPIRITUAL DISCIPLINES

1. Elton T. Trueblood, *The New Man for Our Time,* quoted in Rueben P. Job and Norman Shawchuck, *A Guide to Prayer for All God's People* (Nashville: The Upper Room, 1990), 250.
2. Richard J. Foster, *Prayer: Finding the Heart's True Home* (San Francisco: HarperSanFrancisco, 1992), 67.
3. Brother Lawrence, *The Practice of the Presence of God* (New York: Image Books, Doubleday, 1977), 48-49.

WEEK EIGHT: PLANT THE WORD IN YOUR HEART AND MIND

1. Charles Stanley, *A Touch of His Peace* (Grand Rapids: Zondervan Publishing House, 1993), 81.

WEEK NINE: PURSUE HOLINESS

1. Jerry Bridges, *The Practice of Godliness* (Colorado Springs: Navpress, 1983), 148.
2. Jerry Bridges, *The Pursuit of Holiness* (Colorado Springs: Navpress, 1978), 40-41.
3. Ibid., 71.
4. Ibid.
5. Ibid., 74.
6. Charles Stanley, *A Touch of His Peace* (Grand Rapids: Zondervan Publishing House, 1993), 81.
7. Ibid., 125.
8. Bridges, *Practice of Godliness,* 156-57.
9. Ibid., 158.

WEEK TEN: PLACE YOURSELF IN GOD'S PRESENCE

1. Brother Lawrence, *The Practice of the Presence of God* (New York: Image Books, Doubleday, 1977), 9-10.
2. Ibid., 101.

3. Ibid., 41, 49.

4. Ibid., 40.

5. Ibid., 101, 68.

6. Ibid., 104

7. Ibid., 101-02.

8. Ibid., 102.

9. Ibid., 103.

WEEK ELEVEN: PRESENT YOURSELF FOR SERVICE

1. Jean-Pierre De Caussade, *The Sacrament of the Present Moment* (San Francisco: Harper & Row Publishers, 1982), 9. (Chapter 11 was based on this book.)

2. Thomas Merton, *New Seeds of Contemplation,* quoted in Rueben P. Job and Norman Shawchuck, *A Guide to Prayer for All God's People* (Nashville: The Upper Room, 1990), 354.

3. Stephen D. Bryant, "Letter to a Friend," *Weavings,* (May/June 1989), 355.

4. Elisabeth Elliot, *A Slow and Certain Light: Some Thoughts on the Guidance of God* (Waco: Word Books, Publishers, 1973), 50.

5. Richard J. Foster, *Celebration of Discipline: The Path to Spiritual Growth* (San Francisco: Harper & Row, Publishers, 1978), 80.

6. Elliot, *Slow and Certain Light,* 88, 89, 90.

7. Ibid., 52.

8. Ibid., 95-96.

WEEK TWELVE: PRESS ON IN PAINFUL CIRCUMSTANCES

1. John R. Aurelio, *Mosquitoes in Paradise* (New York: Ballantine Books, 1985), 101.

2. Elisabeth Kubler-Ross, *On Death- and Dying* (New York: Macmillan Publishing Company, 1969), 38-137.

WEEK THIRTEEN: PREPARE FOR A SPIRITUAL RETREAT

1. Rueben P. Job and Norman Shawchuck, *A Guide to Prayer for All God's People* (Nashville: The Upper Room, 1990), 17.

2. Ibid., 18.

WEEK FOURTEEN: PROMISE TO FOLLOW THE LORD

1. E. W. Blandy, John S. Norris, "Where He Leads Me," *Praise! Our Songs and Hymns* (Grand Rapids: Singspiration of the Zondervan Corporation, 1979), 454.

2. Henry F. Lyte, Wolfgang A. Mozart, "Jesus, I My Cross Have Taken," Ibid., 447.

3. Mary Brown, Charles E. Prior, Carrie Rounsefell, "I'll Go Where You Want Me to Go," Ibid., 513.

INDEX

Personal Notes

Notes

Notes

Notes

_____

_____

_____

_____

_____

_____

_____

_____

_____

_____

_____

_____

_____

_____

_____

_____

_____

_____

_____

_____

_____

_____

Notes

Notes